The T-Form Organization

Henry C. Lucas, Jr.

The T-Form Organization

Using Technology to Design Organizations for the 21st Century

Jossey-Bass Publishers • San Francisco

Discussion of Rosenbluth Travel (Chapter Four, pages 80–83) from *Information Systems Concepts for Management* (5th ed., 1994) by H. Lucas, Jr. Used by permission of McGraw-Hill, Inc.

Table 6.1 and the description, from "Reengineering: A Framework for Evaluation and Case Study of an Imaging System," appear courtesy of ACM., Inc., to be published in a forthcoming issue of *Communications of the ACM,* copyright © 1995.

Substantial discounts on bulk quantities of Jossey-Bass books are available to corporations, professional associations, and other organizations. For details and discount information, contact the special sales department at Jossey-Bass Inc., Publishers. (415) 433–1740; Fax (800) 605–2665.

For sales outside the United States, please contact your local Simon & Schuster International Office.

TCF Manufactured in the United States of America on Lyons Falls Pathfinder Tradebook. This paper is acid-free and 100 percent totally chlorine-free.

Library of Congress Cataloging-in-Publication Data

Lucas, Henry C.
    The T-form organization : using technology to design organizations for the 21st century / Henry C. Lucas, Jr. — 1st ed.
       p.   cm. — (The Jossey-Bass management series)
    Includes bibliographical references (p.   ) and index.
    ISBN 0–7879–0167–9
    1. Industrial organization—Forecasting. 2. Reengineering (Management)—Forecasting. 3. Communication in organizations—Technological innovations. 4. Information technology. 5. Twenty-first century—Forecasts. I. Title. II. Series.
HD38.L73   1996
658.4'063—dc20   95–35315

FIRST EDITION
HB Printing   10 9 8 7 6 5 4 3 2 1

The Jossey-Bass Management Series

Consulting Editors
Organizations and Management

Warren Bennis
University of Southern California

Richard O. Mason
Southern Methodist University

Ian I. Mitroff
University of Southern California

To Ellen

Contents

Preface   xi

The Author   xv

Part One: A New Way to Organize   1

1. The T-Form Organization: Flat and Fast   3

2. Building Blocks: The New Design Variables   29

3. Steps Toward Change: Preparation and Pitfalls   53

**Part Two: The Dramatic Impact
of Information Technology**   71

4. Corporate Strategy: Creating the New Road Map
   for Competing   73

5. Virtual Markets: Making Electronic Connections
   with Stakeholders   87

6. Radical Change: Redesigning the Organization   101

Part Three: Designing the T-Form Organization   123

7. Technology-Based Structures: New Organizational
   Forms   125

8. Information-Based Operations: New Ways to
   Do Business   139

9. Customer-Based Service: A New Focus for Business   151

10. Group-Based Communications: Changing the
    Way We Manage   165

    Part Four: Building the Technology Infrastructure   **179**

11. Networks: The Ubiquitous Electronic Alliance   181

12. Technologies: The Future That Is Already Here   197

    Part Five: Implementing the T-Form Design   **213**

13. The Challenge of Change: Converting from Old
    to New Design   215

14. The T-Form Reconsidered: Pathways to Success and
    Competitiveness   229

    Glossary   239

    References   247

    Index   251

Preface

For centuries, managers have designed organizations. Over time, the most popular organization structure has been a hierarchy, much like an army's chain of command. To compete in the twenty-first century, however, organizations will have to be far more flexible than a hierarchical structure allows them to be. In fact, *the traditional organization that fails to redesign itself in the next decade is likely to disappear.*

In designing organization structures, managers have used such concepts as span of control, authority versus responsibility, reporting relationships, formal communications channels, and similar concepts. They have also designed departures from a strict hierarchy; for example, professional service firms are structured somewhat differently than are most manufacturing companies. However, no matter in what industry we look, most businesses essentially consist of layers of managers with well-defined reporting relationships.

Yet this picture is now starting to change. During the last forty years, we have experienced a revolution in information technology (IT), a revolution that will equal or exceed the industrial revolution in its impact on business. In the early days of computers, we could hardly call technology revolutionary. However, computers and communications technologies have evolved into powerful and sophisticated tools, and some managers are now using these tools to create radically different types of organizations.

The purpose of this book is to show managers how they can use information technology, combined with conventional design approaches, to create a technology-based organization, the *T-Form organization*. This book is intended for managers of all types of organizations, including manufacturing firms, service companies, and nonprofits. While senior managers are heavily involved in designing organizations, managers at all levels make decisions that affect the structure of the organization and the design of the work; thus the ideas presented in this book should help a wide range of managers design organizations and their components. There have been many books written recently about networked organizations, virtual organizations, and similar "businesses of the future." This book goes beyond description; its unique contribution is a focus on the IT design variables that managers can use to develop a T-Form organization. A *design variable* affects organizational form once it is applied in the organization. For example, through the design variable of *electronic communications and linking*, you can create an organization in which your employees do not work together in a physical office. This book shows you how to use design variables in a step-by-step process to produce variations of the T-Form organization.

Overview of the Contents

In Part One, I introduce the T-Form organization. Chapter One describes the characteristics of this new form. Given the capabilities of modern information technology, how will successful organizations be structured in the future? Chapter Two presents conventional design variables and the new variables for design based on information technology. This chapter is key to building the T-Form organization. Chapter Three discusses how to prepare to design a new organization and the pitfalls you may encounter; it is especially concerned with creating and maintaining flexibility in organizations.

It is important to understand the full impact of IT on the business environment if we are to design our organizations around it. I address this topic in Part Two. In Chapter Four, we see how technology has affected corporate strategy, while Chapter Five looks at the organizational implications of electronic markets. There is much excitement today about business process redesign or *reengineering*; Chapter Six presents a detailed example of using technology to reengineer a process. It then expands that concept to one of reengineering the entire organization, something that may be necessary if you want to develop the T-Form organization quickly rather than over a long period of time.

In Part Three, I show how to apply the IT design variables from Chapter Two to the design of the T-Form organization. Chapter Seven describes how to use IT to change the structure of an organization. Chapters Eight and Nine focus on technology to change operations and customer service, respectively. Chapter Ten is devoted to groupware, a communications tool that many organizational consultants and managers feel will be one of the most important contributions information technology will make to organizations. IT gives managers unprecedented abilities to share data and to create a repository of a firm's knowledge for many employees to access.

The technology infrastructure is of particular importance when using IT design variables. In Part Four, I discuss computers, communications, and networks—the technologies that have made IT design variables possible. Chapter Eleven describes the dramatically expanding reach of the networks that enable the T-Form organization. Chapter Twelve discusses the kind of technology that is available for building the T-Form organization; almost everything needed is here today at a reasonable price!

Change is never easy, and the last part of this book discusses implementation. The most favorable situation you can be in, of course, is starting a new firm. It is a formidable challenge to move to the T-Form in a large bureaucratic organization. Chapter Thirteen presents some ideas for creating the T-Form organization and describes approaches to using IT design variables successfully. Finally, Chapter Fourteen reviews IT design variables, advantages of the T-Form structure, and steps in creating the T-Form organization. A short glossary explains some of the technical terms used in the book.

Throughout, you will find numerous examples that illustrate how different firms have used IT design variables to design parts of a T-Form organization. Some of these examples, unlike those in many other books, are presented in extensive detail. For each suggestion I make about how to use an IT design variable, I present examples of one or more companies that have successfully employed that variable, for example, to dramatically improve operations or customer service.

My objective is to convince you that information technology design variables provide an exciting new set of tools for creating dynamic, flexible, and responsive organizations, and that when you combine IT and conventional design variables, the most natural outcome is a T-Form organization. I believe that firms that fail to take advantage of IT design variables to evolve toward a T-Form structure are unlikely to survive the turbulent global business environment of the coming years. The challenge for the manager is clear; I have written this book to help you meet it.

Acknowledgments

I gratefully acknowledge Jack Baroudi at New York University for his contributions to developing the IT design variables in Chapter Two. Jon Turner at New York University provided a superb account of Oticon, a company discussed in Chapter Six.

I would also like to thank Jossey-Bass editors Dick Mason, Bill Hicks, and Byron Schneider for their insightful comments and editorial work on this book.

I am forever grateful to my wife, Ellen, for her continued support and encouragement of my writing efforts.

Summit, New Jersey   Henry C. Lucas, Jr.
August 1995

The Author

Henry C. Lucas, Jr., is research professor of information systems at the Leonard N. Stern School of Business, New York University. He received his B.S. degree (1966) from Yale University and both his M.S. degree (1968) and Ph.D. degree in management (1970) from the Sloan School of Management at M.I.T. Lucas has served on the faculty of the Graduate School of Business at Stanford University and has visited at the European Institute of Business Administration (INSEAD) in Fontainebleau, France. He has also done research at the IBM European Systems Research Institute in La Hulpe, Belgium, and at Bell Communications Research in Morristown, New Jersey.

Lucas's research interests include the management and implementation of information technology, systems analysis, expert systems, and the impact of technology. His articles have been published in journals such as *Management Science*, *Decision Science*, the *Sloan Management Review*, *MIS Quarterly*, and the *Journal of Organizational Computing*.

Lucas has authored several books, including *Managing Information Services* (1989), *The Analysis, Design, and Implementation of Information Systems* (4th ed., 1992), and *Information Systems Concepts for Management* (5th ed., 1994).

The T-Form Organization

Part One

A New Way to Organize

The last four decades have brought dramatic social and economic changes, including the rise of the global firm, the movement of the countries of the former Soviet Union and Eastern Europe toward free market economies, and the surge in the economies of China and the rest of Asia. Concomitantly with these globally important changes, there has been a revolution in information technology (IT). For businesses, the end result from these events has been and continues to be tremendous new opportunities along with significant competitive pressures.

Evidence for the intense competition can be seen in the fate of blue-chip companies in the United States: firms like General Motors, IBM, Westinghouse, Digital Equipment Corporation, and others have experienced dramatic reversals. Dissatisfied stockholders and boards of directors have replaced senior management in each of these firms, and the new managers have undertaken extensive restructurings. It is likely that the IBM of the year 2000 will have less than half the number of employees it had in the 1980s!

While large companies have encountered significant problems in remaining competitive, the economy in the United States has offered tremendous opportunities for new companies, particularly those that have learned to take advantage of information technology. Since they do not begin with the kind of multilayer bureaucracy typical of an IBM or a General Motors, these companies have been able to experiment with different kinds of organization structures. Certainly, we cannot compare small start-up companies with the world's largest manufacturing organizations on most fronts, but we have to wonder if these entrepreneurial firms have discovered a new way to organize themselves. Suspicion that there may be a better way to organize is heightened when we look at some large firms or at some divisions of very large firms that also have found more effective ways to compete. Information technology has contributed to many of the benefits certain organizations have enjoyed from their restructuring efforts.

Part One introduces the T-Form, or technology-based, organization. Chapter One describes how information technology can help managers design an organization with the features needed to compete in today's economy: for example, a "flat" organization structure, with few layers of management. Chapter Two presents a series of IT design variables, building blocks to be combined with traditional organization design variables to create variations of the T-Form organization. The third chapter describes how to prepare to design or redesign an organization. It also points out potential pitfalls on the road to the T-Form organization.

Is the effort required to design a new technology-based organization worth it? Mangers may have little choice; *I believe that firms will have to adopt the T-Form organization to survive in the highly competitive global economy of the twenty-first century.*

Chapter One

The T-Form Organization: Flat and Fast

The revolution in information technology during the last forty years offers managers new ways to design highly efficient, competitive organizations. Many experts have speculated on the impact of information technology on organization design. As long ago as 1958, Leavitt and Whisler predicted significant changes in organizations as a result of new IT. They stated: "Over the last decade [the 1950s] a new technology has begun to take hold in American business, one so new that its significance is still difficult to evaluate. While many aspects of this technology are uncertain, it seems clear that it will move into the managerial scene rapidly, with definite and far-reaching impact on managerial organization" (p. 41). Many of the changes Leavitt and Whisler predicted, such as reductions in the number of management layers and in the total number of middle managers, are now taking place.

It is hard to select one particular organization form and claim that it represents *the* structure of the future. There are hundreds of thousands of organizations, and it is unlikely that a manufacturing company will develop a structure that looks exactly like that of a law firm. However, we do know that technology makes certain organizational forms attractive and that there are pressures moving organizations in particular new directions. The combination of these external pressures and the new technology has the potential to change the way firms are structured, and the shape of these changes, at least, can be defined.

Information Technology and Organization Design

The purpose of this book is to describe how managers can use information technology to design new organizations or redesign existing ones. It presents a series of new information technology design variables to be used in creating a technology-based, or *T-Form*, organization. A number of examples illustrate how these technology-based variables can be used to design the T-Form organization that is appropriate for each firm's unique business environment.

My basic argument is that the information technology developed during the last four decades, particularly communications networks and software to support individuals and groups in their tasks, not only can be used but must be used in organization design. *Ideally, instead of designing an organization and adding IT later, managers will use technology actively in designing their organizations in the first place.* I believe that now and in the years to come, T-Form businesses will significantly outperform firms with more traditional organization structures. Indeed, it will be a rare traditionally structured organization that survives in the twenty-first century.

What has happened to make IT a vital element in designing organizations? The first information systems processed basic transactions, often where there was intense paperwork. These systems handled orders, billing, accounting, and production control; improving the processing of this paperwork made a significant contribution to successful operations. In the last five years, however, some organizations have found ways to employ technology that go well beyond simple transaction-processing applications. Out of the convergence of communications and computer technologies, they have created new opportunities in the way work is organized. The first transaction-processing systems altered workflows and tasks for one department or a small group of departments. Today's technology provides managers with opportunities to create new structures for entire organizations.

In the next chapter, I examine the new IT organization design variables. While many firms are currently employing one or a few of these variables, I am unaware of an organization that has taken full advantage of IT in designing or restructuring itself. It is my hope that this book will help companies see many more of the opportunities that information technology offers them.

The T-Form Organization

What are the characteristics of the T-Form, or technology-based, organization? The manager who designs this new type of organization has a great deal of freedom in choosing its structure. IT organization design variables can be used in a number of different ways. But given the objective that most firms have today of being highly efficient and minimizing overhead, I suggest that most managers will employ technology to produce an organization with a relatively flat structure—that is, a structure that has a minimum number of layers of management. The classical approach to organization design stresses concepts such as span of control. How many subordinates can a supervisor manage? Numbers like seven or eight are popular answers to this question. Other designers use a pragmatic standard, saying, "When a person has too much work to do, we provide him or her with subordinates to help out."

Instituting a rigid span of control and providing subordinates whenever needed are very expensive ways to design organizations. By following these design variables over the years, firms have built up huge bureaucracies that are very costly to support. The T-Form organization substitutes technology for layers of management. First, communications technology demolishes the old idea of span of control: now, a manager can stay in contact with and "supervise" a large number of subordinates electronically. Of course, compared to the close supervision made possible by sitting near one's subordinates, this supervision will be more remote and will require much more trust between manager and subordinate.

Second, technology, not more subordinates, can be used to help the manager perform his or her tasks. The kinds of support available through a personal computer workstation connected to a network make a manager far more productive today than in the past.

Another objective for today's corporation is to remain flexible. Market needs and business conditions change rapidly. A firm has to respond quickly to these changes, a characteristic not associated with large bureaucracies. IBM presents a good example of the inertia generated in an entrenched bureaucracy. The company remained oblivious to industry trends toward smaller, more powerful computers until the mainframe market crumbled.

The T-Form organization uses matrix management and temporary work groups to create much-needed flexibility. Matrix management allows multiple assignments to be given to staff members. The field of information technology itself has used this structure for many years. Systems analysts and programmers typically work on more than one project at a time. They report both to a project manager for each project and to an overall manager of systems and programming.

Matrix management was popular twenty years ago but seems to have fallen out of favor, except in naturally team-oriented activities like systems development. One reason may be that matrix management is more complex than the typical hierarchical form of management. Also, employees sometimes find multiple reporting relationships unsettling. Today, however, electronic communications are making it easier to form task forces of employees who cut across a number of functional areas of a business. In fact, it is likely that these task forces will even include individuals from external organizations. The engineer designing a new automobile, for example, will include personnel from outside parts suppliers on the design team.

Technology alone is not enough to produce the T-Form organization; to take advantage of IT as it is introduced, the culture and climate of the organization have to change. In addition to forming matrices and temporary task forces, management has to decentralize decision making if the organization is to achieve flexibility. Flexibility depends in part on good and quick problem solving, and firms have found that managers closest to a problem are in the best position to solve it. Technology makes it possible to provide managers at any level in the firm with the information they need for problem solving; once individuals close to the problem have that information, management has to be willing to delegate decision making to them. By this, I mean that the management gives the individual the authority to commit the organization and/or its resources *without prior approval*. If you are that individual, you may have to report on your actions, but you will only rarely be overruled, and you are free to act without checking with someone else first.

The presence of delegated, decentralized decision making implies that organizational members possess a high level of trust. Members of top management must have faith in managers at all levels in the firm, and they must believe that the information systems in place provide the appropriate information for managers to take action. Trust, then, is an essential part of the culture in a T-Form organization.

Another characteristic of the T-Form organization is that it is less concerned with its physical structure than with its logical structure. What you perceive may not be exactly what is there! We are all used to organizations housed in an identifiable location; these firms have well-defined organization charts that show where everyone reports. The T-Form organization may appear to be a traditionally structured firm while its actual physical structure relies on communications technology like electronic mail (e-mail), groupware, and distributed offices, providing the firm with more flexibility than the traditional structure ever did. Reporting relationships can and will change as the T-Form firm faces new demands.

There are other reasons than flexibility to eliminate old-fashioned notions of physical location and rigid organization charts. Employers in Los Angeles found that they had little choice but to open satellite offices after the 1994 earthquake; critical freeways were closed, and employees could not get to work at a central location. In addition, clean air requirements in many cities will force employees to work at home or at satellite offices to reduce commuting in the twenty-first century.

One of the major business and technological trends in the last part of the twentieth century has been the development of interorganizational systems (IOS). Companies have established electronic links with their customers and suppliers. From the late 1960s on, when American Hospital Supply encouraged its customers to connect to its order entry computer system, firms have been forging electronic links with the organizations with whom they do business.

At first, these links focused on routine, well-specified transactions. Electronic data interchange (EDI) has proven very effective in a variety of industries, including trucking, auto manufacturing, and retailing. In addition to managing routine customers and suppliers transactions, however, firms can easily establish electronic mail and groupware connectivity with external organizations in order to work more closely on a continual basis with those customers and suppliers. Electronic communications facilitate such close relationships.

One of the most popular topics today is "process reengineering," a topic I cover in more detail in Chapter Six. Reengineering focuses management attention on business processes, regardless of the department or functions that might have partial responsibility for a process. An order entry system, for example, cuts across a number of departments from order taking to inventory control to the warehouse. Instead of looking at the work of each of these functions as a separate task, process engineering concentrates on the order-cycle process itself. In the T-Form organization, also, functional organization is becoming less important. The T-Form firm identifies its processes and has process "owners" who are responsible for seeing that the process works.

The T-Form organization has a number of *virtual components*. A virtual component is a company function that exists physically in a traditional organization but that has been replaced by a electronic version in the T-Form organization. In the late 1980s, Chrysler Corporation moved to a just-in-time (JIT) production process with its suppliers. A JIT firm runs with less than a day's supply of raw materials and work-in-process inventory. The auto manufacturer estimates that it eliminated a billion dollars worth of inventory throughout its system by going to JIT. Where does that inventory go? It exists in a different form in the information systems that let Chrysler suppliers know exactly what to produce and when to deliver it to a Chrysler plant.

Baxter Healthcare offers a stockless service to hospitals. Baxter delivers medical supplies to the department that needs them on a just-in-time basis. Each hospital has a virtual inventory that is kept and supplied by Baxter. Virtual components are an important part of the T-Form organization; they are responsible for much of its efficiency and flexibility.

A step beyond the virtual component is the *virtual organization*. The virtual organization can be created through a negotiated agreement with another firm. Baxter's stockless inventory service involves a negotiated agreement with each customer. In Chapter Seven, I look at Calyx & Corolla, a direct-sales flower company that has negotiated agreements with growers to supply flower arrangements and with Federal Express to provide delivery services.

These types of agreements represent a new form of *strategic alliance* with other corporations. Baxter and Calyx & Corolla have intertwined their production, logistics, and even their marketing functions with other organizations to create what looks like a single traditional organization to the customer. Note that such an alliance implies more than just a make-or-buy decision; the firm is purchasing more than a component to plug into some part of its organization. An alliance involves a pooling of interests, not a one-time purchase or sale. The firms in an alliance become interdependent and form a partnership; each is interested in the success of the other.

An alliance lets each firm do what it does best; that is, each firm operates where it has a comparative advantage. A trend in today's business, after many companies diversified or bought other firms, is to return to one's "core competence." Xerox, for example, sold its financial services divisions to concentrate once again on being a document-processing company. It would not make much sense for Federal Express to acquire firms in order to ship those firms' products. The FedEx core competence is in running a first-class delivery and transportation system. It can be a strategic partner with a number of businesses, as it is with Calyx & Corolla.

Since the T-Form organization is heavily based on information technology, another of its characteristic is the ability to successfully manage IT. While this observation may seem obvious, I am struck by the number of firms who depend on IT but do a very poor job of managing that technology. This book is not about IT management, but the reader should be aware of how important it is for managers to understand and participate in the decisions their organizations make about technology. Management cannot just delegate technology decisions to others; management must take an active part in shaping and managing IT. Technology is too important to be left to technologists.

Finally, the effective T-Form organization is characterized by a technology infrastructure; that is, it has adequate technology in place to take advantage of new opportunities. The infrastructure includes components such as a communications network for voice and data and networked workstations for all managers, support staff, and a variety of production workers. It is difficult, if not impossible, to cost justify all infrastructure investments in advance. In fact, traditional capital budgeting techniques like net present value do not seem to work very well when applied to infrastructure investments.

But a communications network is necessary because it connects everyone in the firm. It allows the flexible organization structures described above. This network will soon be *intelligent*, populated with *agents* that will do tasks for the manager the way a robot does tasks for the factory worker. Software to support workgroups is also an important component of the T-Form organization, even though a direct and short-run return from that kind of investment is also very difficult to demonstrate.

Figure 1.1 sums up all the aspects of the T-Form organization introduced here.

The Role of People

This book is about using IT to design organizations; much of the discussion is, therefore, about structures rather than people. Yet organizations consist of individuals who occupy different positions

Figure 1.1. The T-Form Organization.

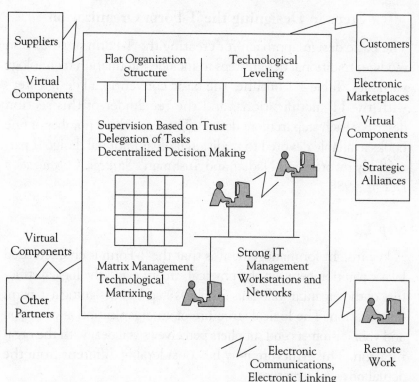

in a structure, and the characteristics of the T-Form organization, especially decentralized decision making, responsiveness, lack of bureaucracy, and a minimum of management layers, influence the way people feel about their companies and jobs.

Traditional organizations often stifle creativity and frustrate employees. One objective of the T-Form organization is to create an environment in which employees can excel. Managers in a T-Form organization have to trust employees and give them significant responsibility. Employees who accept the challenge can expand their horizons and learn new skills, for example, through work on matrixed project teams, expanded communications with customers, and new relationships with suppliers. The T-Form organization helps employees maximize their contributions to the firm and enjoy the satisfaction that comes with being able to perform well.

Steps in Designing the T-Form Organization

The basic design approach for creating the T-Form organization modifies traditional design steps to include information technology variables. Table 1.1 outlines the basic conventional design steps with the IT modifications, and the remainder of this section describes each step in more detail. (There are also a number of fine books available devoted to traditional organizational design. I particularly recommend Nadler and Tushman's *Strategic Organization Design*, 1988.)

Step 1

A key insight for management is that the T-Form is characterized by a separation between the physical structure and the logical structure of the organization. This insight is step 1 in designing a T-Form organization. The logical structure of an organization is what you and your customers and suppliers perceive as you deal with the organization. This structure may be considerably different from the actual physical structure.

Table 1.1. Steps in the Design of the T-Form Organization.

Design Step	Comments
1. Recognize that the physical and logical structures of an organization are separate.	This insight lets you develop virtual components, minimize layers of management, and so on.
2. Develop a corporate strategy.	You still need to consider strategy in designing an organization for the twenty-first century.
3. Identify processes.	Process redesign can bring major efficiencies.
4. Integrate classical design steps with IT design variables.	We can learn from classic design, but IT should be an integral part of the design, not an "add on."
5. Design the logical structure of the organization.	The logical structure is how the organization appears to the external world; it is usually the traditional view people have of organizations.
6. Design the physical structure of the organization.	Physical structure is defined by communications patterns, task forces, informal groups, alliances with outside organizations, and "virtual" components.
7. Plan for temporary task forces and matrix management.	This strategy provides flexibility and a capability for fast reorganization.
8. Focus on key decisions that provide choice in organization design.	Examples include forming an alliance with a supplier or customer.
9. Design tasks.	Tasks may be designed by those who perform them or by experts in the work function.

**Table 1.1. Steps in the Design
of the T-Form Organization, Cont'd.**

Design Step	Comments
10. Build or buy a technology infrastructure.	The firm needs to have a variety of technology in place.
11. Use compensation policy to help achieve goals.	Some compensation should be based on the performance of the organization.
12. Trust workers and lead through influence.	Large spans of control, remote workers, and temporary task forces require that managers trust the work force.

For example, Lithonia Lighting, a company that makes a variety of lighting fixtures, primarily for the construction industry, has a number of physical divisions to make its different kinds of lights; however, when Lithonia redesigned its information systems, one of its goals was to make the company look like one single organization to customers. Lithonia did not want a customer to contact one part of the organization for lighting for an athletic field and another part for fluorescent office lights. Today, a customer can order any or all of Lithonia's products by calling one central phone number. A single order entry system processes all orders and decides where to send them to be filled. Information technology makes it possible for Lithonia to create a logical view of the organization for customers that is different from Lithonia's actual physical divisions and manufacturing plants.

The opportunities offered by information technology suggest that managers in the twenty-first century will want to:

- Minimize the number of layers of management.
- Develop virtual components.
- Link to customers and suppliers.

- Form temporary project teams and task forces.
- Form alliances with other organizations.

In the flexible organization formed by separating the logical and the physical structure, management should be able to restructure easily to achieve a new strategy. Conversely, traditional bureaucracies have great difficulty responding to shifts in strategy.

Step 2

As its second general design step, a firm needs to develop its corporate strategy, which will influence how the firm is structured and how it allocates technology resources. A firm that has chosen customer service as its strategy, for example, will allocate more IT investment to its customer service function than to other parts of the organization and will spend more time designing that function.

Today, we can observe a number of corporate strategies followed by different major firms; there are undoubtedly others. Just as this is not a text on the management of IT, neither is it a text on corporate strategy. However, I do discuss corporate strategies somewhat further in Chapter Three because certain aspects of strategy drive technology investment and organization design. These aspects of strategy include:

- Right-sizing
- A focus on the customer
- A focus on quality
- Cycle time reduction
- Going global

Step 3

I have mentioned the attention that reengineering has focused on business processes. Corporations have obtained impressive results from redesigning processes, so as step 3, it seems logical to identify critical processes as part of organizational design. You may still want to have functional groupings for many purposes, but a process "owner" who cuts across functional groups should be in charge of major business processes.

Step 4

In designing the T-Form organization, there is nothing wrong with considering the traditional approaches to organization design. However, the traditional method tends to omit information technology design variables. IT then becomes something that is added on to make improvements after the organization has been designed. Step 4 of designing a T-Form organization, and a fundamental lesson of this book, is to consider traditional and IT organization design variables *simultaneously* in structuring the organization.

Step 5

Step 5 is to design the logical structure of the organization, that is, as explained earlier, the structure that the external world sees. The logical structure also identifies what processes and functions need to be performed. As a result of its logical design, a company of many parts may look like one monolithic organization to customers placing an order. It may appear to have a number of internal departments when, in fact, the departmental functions are performed by external organizations. The raw materials inventory might exist on a suppliers' premises rather than in the manufacturer's own factory. But the logical structure is the organization chart customers or other outsiders would draw if asked to describe the firm.

Step 6

Step 6 is to design the physical structure of the organization. The logical design of your organization identifies what processes and functions need to be performed while the physical design determines how the organization realizes the logical view. Again, you may substitute alliances with external firms for internal departments. Instead of developing a complex logistics and distribution system, you may contract with a carrier like United Parcel Service or Federal Express to handle all deliveries. A common centralized order entry computer can accept orders for a number of different plants. Some of these plants may not even be part of your formal organization! In developing the physical structure of the organization, managers rely heavily on the information technology design variables described in detail in Chapter Two.

Step 7

If you build a T-Form organization, expect to plan for both temporary workgroups and permanent and temporary matrix management as step 7. Here again, communications technologies make it easy to form and manage these groups, groups that can span large physical distances. Will members ever meet? It is a good idea for workgroups to have physical meetings, but the number of meetings can be significantly reduced through electronic communications. As videoconferencing becomes more widespread and people can see each other electronically as well as exchange messages, the need for physical meetings will drop even further.

Step 8

When designing an organization, it is important to ask the questions that have a major impact on organization structure—questions such as should we make or buy this product or service, or how should we deliver our product? There may be a good reason to establish a transportation division to handle all product deliveries. However, you may also want to consider a virtual distribution network formed through an electronic alliance with an overnight carrier. Step 8 is the time when you make sure the key decisions your organization makes are guiding your design.

Step 9

In step 9, the organization designer helps determine how tasks will be performed. In many instances, the details of task performance will be left up to the individual assigned the task. In other instances, for example, the design of a production line, experts will be needed. Engineers and managers together will design tasks for many production operations, both in manufacturing and in service.

Step 10

As mentioned earlier, you need a technology infrastructure to facilitate the creation of the T-Form organization. Acquiring this infrastructure is step 10. The minimum components of the infrastructure include:

- Routine transaction-processing systems: today's managers cannot afford the costs, errors, and lack of information that go along with processing routine transactions manually.
- Workstations for managers and other employees: managers and many employees need a full complement of business software: spreadsheets, database management software, word processors, presentation graphics, mail systems, groupware, and connections to external networks.
- Internal and external networking capabilities: much of the T-Form organization's success depends on employees' ability to network with one another and with members of external firms. The most popular architecture for this purpose today is a client-server network in which multiple computers provide programs and data for users connected to the network through their workstations. Because networks can interconnect, a single workstation can access departmental data on a local server, groupware databases on an organizational server, and external networks that connect with suppliers and customers.

- Data retrieval and analysis capabilities: managers will want to have a variety of decision support systems, executive information systems, statistical packages, and connections to external services that provide economic and competitive data.

Step 11

One of the most important traditional managerial variables is compensation. Its importance continues in the T-Form organization. Step 11 is to use compensation policy as one means of achieving corporate goals. You need to base some part of people's compensation on overall company performance or some aspect of that performance. For example, sales and service personnel might be compensated partially on customer satisfaction. Partially basing compensation on other appropriate aspects of behavior might be used to encourage collaboration, team leadership, and the like.

Step 12

Finally, as mentioned earlier, senior managers have to trust employees. You need independent action and decision making by all employees. The autocrat who makes all decisions and closely monitors subordinates will not be able to function in a T-Form organization. Management needs to encourage informal communications and initiative. The T-Form organization is lean; managers no longer have a large number of subordinates with whom to discuss decisions or multiple committees to delay a decision. The employee in the T-Form organization can seek advice electronically and then he or she will act quickly to deal with the competitive environment. Therefore, managers in the T-Form organization must trust and support their subordinates in decision making.

There is another important role for managers in the T-Form organization—they must provide leadership. The manager recognizes his or her responsibility for organization design and sees that he or she acts on it. The manager has to implement a new design and monitor its impact on the organization. The examples of design in this book show the results of a number of bold initiatives on the part of managers. That kind of leadership is not simply one of the steps in design; it is a constant force in conceptualizing and implementing any new organization design.

Scenario from a Twenty-First Century Firm

One way to stimulate your thoughts about the organization of the future is to look at a scenario for what might be available in a few years. What will the technology make possible? What could you do if you wanted to design a radically different organization using that technology? The following scenario is based on the work of Jarvenpaa and Ives (1994). It is set ten to fifteen years into the future, and it depicts organizational life for the Worldwide Group, a management consulting firm. We spend an evening with a wide-roving consultant faced with the task of executing a marketing initiative in less than eighteen hours.

The landing gear of the 787 came up as Tara Rodgers in seat 6B linked her personal assistant to an onboard computer built into the armrest of her seat. The display screen on the back of the seat in front of her was larger and had a higher resolution than the screen on Tara's personal assistant. It also provided access to the airline's electronic amenities. Tara tuned into the airline's audio system, which gave her capabilities similar to those of her personal assistant, including connection to inflight entertainment, the ability to listen to ground control conversations, and special circuitry to eliminate the plane's background noise.

Tara touched an icon on the screen in front of her to view the inflight service menu. She canceled dinner, eliminated nonessential messages from flight personnel (Tara had taken the flight many times before and did not want the captain's sight-seeing instructions). She asked for a glass of port to be delivered in two hours. She did not expect her electronic documents to attract the attention of the EUC's customs and immigration systems, but she authorized the system to wake her if an onboard interview with immigration officials was requested. By speaking softly into a microphone plugged into the armrest, Tara completed her customs declaration. The airlines' computers had already entered the flight number, date, and other details of the trip.

Tara barely noticed the soft, classical music that she had chosen as background for her audio system. Her personal profile, stored in her assistant, or possibly the airline's frequent flyer database, had chosen her type of music and preset the volume based on her personal preferences. This profile would also suggest that her morning coffee be served with cream and no sugar.

Tara touched another icon to make arrangements for her brief stay in Oxford. Her trip from New York was sudden, and she had not made hotel reservations. The electronic reservation agent her firm subscribed to had booked her into a charming guest house she had liked during her last visit to Oxford. Using the travel agent's virtual reality simulator, she wandered into the rooms with open doors (available this evening) and selected the one with the best view of the college. She also could have looked at a short video segment showing where to meet the car she had booked electronically that would take her from Heathrow to Oxford. Had she been closer to London, she could have looked at a prerecorded introduction to her driver.

The airline's computer predicted an on-time arrival with 95 percent certainty, and Tara began the work she wanted to complete before trying to get some sleep. First she called her husband and watched her children at play in their family room.

Back at work, Tara touched a key to activate her electronic messaging system and listened again to the message from the senior partner of Worldwide who had sent her off on this sudden trip. "Tara, this morning I received a message from London from Professor Locke at Templeton College, Oxford. Locke has worked closely with our

U.K. and European offices on a number of projects; London believes he has the inside track on a promising opportunity, but we have to move quickly.

"The prospective customer is Empire Software, a company that specializes in the production of integrated software systems for the international freight business. Sir Phillip Knight, CEO of Empire, is in residence at Templeton College for a three-day forum. Over coffee, Knight expressed a concern to Locke that his firm is not taking advantage of the advances in software engineering and that his management team is poorly prepared to respond to competitive threats. Knight was very interested in some kind of customized educational program for the firm's top 100 employees. Locke has set up a meeting with Knight for tomorrow afternoon at Templeton to talk more. Locke thinks that if we move quickly, we might be able to land this job without Empire's going through a competitive bidding process. Locke would like our help in putting together the educational program.

"Tara, you worked with Knight five years ago on a project when he ran development at Dover Software and you were with that awful competitor of ours. When the U.K. office ran a search, the identifier system came up with your name because of that job and your knowledge of the software industry.

"Empire is a high-growth company that has been very profitable. Locke thinks there will be follow-up business if we get the job. Knight feels Empire is in a bad position to operate globally; he thinks software engineering will help Empire compete. Knight likes the kind of wholesale organizational change program Locke has been talking about in the Templeton seminar. I have checked our customer database and find that we have not done much with Empire, though we have a couple of engagements with them in Asia and Europe. We have no U.S. projects with them.

"I checked your availability for the next two days and have started to reassign your responsibilities to other associates. Jerry Wright is your contact from the London office; he has worked with Locke in the past, but doesn't know Empire or Knight. I contacted

Mary Ellen Smith, who is a doctoral student at the University of California at Irvine, to be your special research assistant. She will be at your disposal for the next forty-eight hours working out of her home. You can ask her to look through our files and external databases to pull together a brief on Empire, their competitors, the industry, and so on."

Tara listened to a forwarded message from Professor Locke and Jerry Wright. She checked corporate records for a profile on Wright; his specialty was working on projects that required pulling together diverse resources from the Worldwide Group. He was highly motivated and would perform, though he might be occasionally a bit brusque and overly task oriented.

Wright had spoken to Locke and forwarded his notes to Tara. Wright had provided the names of several Empire people in the U.S. and Europe that Worldwide was working with. Tara saw that one of these projects pertained to software development productivity. She linked to Worldwide's central databank to review reports on that project. Tara found a presentation prepared and delivered to a technical directions steering committee in Tokyo three months earlier. The findings were similar to Knight's concerns about productivity and global reach. One recommendation was a call for a management education program and an examination of locating a development group in the Pacific Rim.

Tara sent an urgent message to the Tokyo partner who had worked with Empire on this project. He was vacationing on a cruise ship in the Caribbean, but the messaging system located him and forwarded the message in English and Japanese. Tara attached the correspondence relating to her current project and asked for a quick update and one-minute summary of the original findings that she could use the next day. Then she downloaded the complete text of the Tokyo presentation to her personal assistant and highlighted the key sections she would use tomorrow if she did not find better information. Finally, she forwarded the results of her work to Wright in London.

By this time, Mary Ellen Smith had forwarded Tara a dossier on

Empire. Smith had produced a rich assortment of documents on Empire as well as a strong overview report. Using a global paging service, Tara set up a conference call with Smith and an executive education specialist in Boston. Tara wanted a list of names from the firm, from colleges, and from independent consultants of people qualified to participate in a program of this type. She needed data on fees, availability, areas of specialty, and participant evaluations from their past programs. She also wanted to see video clips of each candidate performing in front of an executive audience.

Smith said she would use her electronic agent to search through faculty expertise files in the top-tier business schools around the world. Tara asked Smith to identify five to ten top candidates and the educational specialist to look for several possible venues for the program. Several of the experts would probably remain at their home base and provide instruction through audio, video, and computer links to the conference site. Checking through uploaded files from other Worldwide personal assistants, she found that Knight had a summer home in Bermuda and suggested that as one possible seminar location.

Before signing off, the educational consultant downloaded a multimedia presentation to Tara's personal assistant. Worldwide had recently used this presentation to sell a similar educational project to another client; she could save time by using this "boilerplate" for tomorrow's meeting.

Tara asked the assistant to identify an initial list of individuals who could contribute to the program. Using her firm's database, she checked on their availability over the next six months and watched video clips of several instructors working with executive audiences. She called one presenter in Oregon to ask if she could use his video clip in her presentation tomorrow.

Tara contacted Kolormagic, a firm that provided worldwide graphics work for its clients. Headquartered in Singapore, the company maintained a group of graphic artists around the world who could provide consistent, high-quality multimedia presentations for clients. Singapore offered inducements for the company to locate there, including its superior technology infrastructure.

Kolormagic arranged for an artist on Maui to work with Tara. She checked previous work from this artist in the Worldwide database and was satisfied with his work. She forwarded logos from Worldwide and Empire, names, titles, pictures, and links to the previous multimedia demonstration she had reviewed to the artist. She spent the next hour discussing the presentation with the artist. The artist promised a rough presentation by the time Tara reached Oxford. Locke, Wright, and the Japanese partner in the Caribbean would all be able to review the presentation before it was delivered.

Tara completed a summary of her activities and forwarded it to Wright and the Worldwide database. She set a wakeup call for forty-five minutes before landing. As the flight attendant arrived with the glass of port, she checked Knight's personal profile from her one previous contact with him; she retrieved the name of his favorite wine and forwarded it to Wright in London. Now it was time for some sleep.

The T-Form in Services and Manufacturing

Is this scenario possible? Certainly not today, but it seems feasible, at least in part, in the near future. Later, I discuss some of the technology needed to realize this scenario; the major ingredient to be added to today's computers and communications is greater wireless connectivity and capacity, along with network "intelligence."

In the scenario, the Worldwide group has used technology to create a T-Form organization. The firm has a flat organizational structure and matrix management; consultants work with various managers and project leaders on different assignments. Electronic linking and communications facilitate its matrix management. Technology supports the day-to-day activities of Worldwide employees. The firm features decentralized decision making and temporary task forces to work on problems. There is extensive use of communications technology as people in distributed locations work together without physical interaction. There are electronic links to subcontractors and suppliers. These subcontractors form a virtual global consulting firm through strategic alliances. Finally, Worldwide has a well-developed technology infrastructure.

However, Worldwide is a T-Form professional services firm. Can we also envision a T-Form manufacturing firm? The answer is clearly yes. In the manufacturing scenario, if you are looking for a particular manufactured item, you find it by accessing an electronic marketplace, a nationwide electronic network that contains product descriptions and prices for a host of industrial and consumer products. The easiest way for you to gather information is to send an intelligent software agent to roam networks looking for the items you wish to purchase. Based on the agent's report, you select a manufacturer and inquire electronically about delivery dates.

Satisfied with the quality ratings of the firm and the delivery date, you submit an electronic order. The manufacturing company's computer sends you an electronic acknowledgment and schedules your order for production. As your order began to move into the factory, various suppliers access the manufacturing company's production control system to determine when they need to ship components so they arrive just in time to be added to the product.

The production control system tracks your order through the factory. As each supplier's parts are added to the product, the computer tallies the amount owed to the supplier. At the end of the shift, the manufacturer sends electronic payments to its bank to be credited to each supplier. No paper is exchanged between the manufacturer and its suppliers.

When your product is near completion, the manufacturing firm's computers send your computer an advance notice of shipping; on the day of shipping, the vendor's system notifies your computer and sends information on the carrier and routing. It also sends an electronic statement with a request for payment. Receipt of the product at your loading dock and the completion of an inspection causes your computer to send an electronic payment to the manufacturer through your bank.

Implications

The T-Form is a general organization structure. Each T-Form organization will share such characteristics as a flattened hierarchy, the use of matrix management, technological support of managers, decentralized decision making and temporary task forces, electronic communications, and electronic links with customers and suppliers. However, each organization will also use IT design variables in ways that create a detailed structure that is unique to the firm. The shape of this structure will depend on the nature of the firm's business and the environment in which it operates. For example, technology-supported matrix management at a professional services company might mean that different consultants move around working for different project leaders on different assignments. In a manufacturing company, technology-supported matrix management might have engineers working for both plant and engineering management.

There are many pieces of a modern organization, and managers have a variety of responsibilities. A successful organization design does not necessarily mean that the firm will be successful, though a good design certainly contributes to success. This chapter has described the essential characteristics of that general T-Form organization, a structure likely to be highly successful in the twenty-first century. The next chapter presents information technology design variables that can be used to create or move to a T-Form structure that will exhibit the overall characteristics described in this chapter while also fitting the unique environment of each organization.

Chapter Two

Building Blocks: The New Design Variables

Almost every manager designs organizations! When you decide how secretaries are to be assigned within a department, you are engaged in organization design. Will there be a pool of secretaries, or will each person have a private secretary? A sales manager has to decide how to organize the salesforce. Should it be by product, by customer, by area, or some combination of these items? How should a manager in the information systems area design the organization for systems development? Should the systems staff report to a central information services function, or should staff members report to line managers in different divisions of the company?

Organization design is more than developing a chart of boxes and reporting relationships for a firm. We are involved in organization design whenever we assign tasks to employees, form temporary task forces, realign reporting relationships, and take many other actions that change the way individuals work in a company.

A surprisingly small number of researchers have written about organization design. Henry Mintzberg (1979), for example, gives this simple description of the design process: "Every organized human activity . . . gives rise to two fundamental and opposing requirements: the *division of labor* into various tasks to be performed and the *coordination* of these tasks to accomplish the activity. *The structure of an organization can be defined simply as the sum total of the ways in which it divides its labor into distinct tasks and then achieves coordination among them*" (p. 2, emphasis added). This definition of design is appealing because it is easy to understand, and it focuses on the design of tasks.

Deciding how work will be done is a fundamental job of management. Just looking at tasks and coordination mechanisms, however, does not give managers a good overview of the structure of the complete organization. We often hear a firm described as being organized by product or by line of business, but how does that translate into design options. The next section identifies general design considerations. The remaining sections of this chapter describe the design variables that can be applied to developing the T-Form organization.

Designing the Overall Structure

Nadler and Tushman (1988) address "strategic grouping" in organization design. In their view, the organization has to decide on an overall structure that reflects the firm's strategy, and they see four options. What the company does can be grouped by activity or function, by output, by client or customer, or by multiple foci.

Activity or function. In this structure, people who work in the same function or discipline are grouped together. A Big Six accounting firm, for example, is organized by function: audit, tax, and management services groups are typically found in these firms. Many large bureaucratic firms organize by function. A railroad has an operating division and a "business group." On the one hand, operations has responsibility for running the railroad; it must put together trains and see that they carry freight to the right destination. Operations also has to worry about maintenance of rolling stock and the roadbed. On the other hand, the business group is responsible for marketing, sales, accounting, and interfacing with customers. A similar kind of functional organization can be found in many firms today.

Output. Another structural option is to form groups around output. A large manufacturing company is a good candidate for this kind of organization. General Motors, for example, has divisions that produce different kinds of cars and trucks. It has separate subsidiaries to manufacture products like buses and locomotives. Each of these subunits may have its own marketing, sales, accounting, and other functions that are focused on the output of that subunit.

Client or customer. Strategic grouping by client or customer is typical of a large brokerage firm, which will usually have retail brokers who concentrate on individual investors and institutional brokers who work with professional money managers, such as those who run pension funds. Telephone service companies divide their marketing and sales operation by business and residential customers. If your firm is organized by geography, that is, by where customers are located, you have adopted this kind of strategic structure.

Multiple foci. Some organizations are strategically grouped around several different dimensions. Large organizations, in particular, often exhibit more than one kind of strategic grouping. The typical multinational company may be organized into country units (grouping by customer) and also exhibit a functional organization within each country.

What happens once a company has selected an appropriate strategic orientation for its organization structure? Several authors agree that the next structural task is to think about coordination and linking. All of the four strategic grouping options just described result in some kind of division of labor, some arrangement of divisions, departments, and/or workgroups. A fundamental task of management is to see that the resources of the organization are focused on achieving organizational objectives; therefore, it is generally the case that these groups and their subunits have to be coordinated with the firm's larger objectives.

Next, within each division, department, and workgroup, managers must assign tasks and determine how to achieve the subunit's objectives. This design task involves the design of the work processes themselves. It is clear that the design of work is a major activity in a manufacturing firm, where management may be faced with creating an assembly line or process to produce goods. However, it is also a concern in service industries, where a large number of people are involved in processing different kinds of transactions.

Whatever overall structure the firm takes, one of the important tools available to managers to assist in coordinating and managing the firm and all its parts to achieve its objectives is communications. A communications system is important both inside the firm and outside. If you decide to practice just-in-time manufacturing, for example, you must be able to communicate effectively with the suppliers who will deliver items just as they are needed on the production line. Therefore, communications are also an element that must be designed, along with overall structure and work processes.

Finally, your public relations department, customer service groups, and purchasing department will all have relations with external organizations. You may also be forming strategic alliances and partnerships with other firms. Therefore, you will be called upon to design interorganizational links and communications mechanisms.

The Concept of a Design Variable

How can you arrive at design decisions and execute them? What alternatives are available to you for creating a design? A design variable can take on different values, and these values affect the structure of the organization. An example helps to illustrate the concept of a variable. If you want to compute the annual payment on a loan, you multiply the interest rate by the balance of the loan: payment = interest $\times$ balance (or $P = I \times B$, where I is the interest rate and B is the balance). In this formula, I and B are *variables*; they take on different values for different interest rates and loan balances. They could have any positive value, though in the United States interest rates usually do not exceed 20 percent. Organization design variables also take on different values; for example, companies often have goals for their span of control. Some early management experts recommended a span of control of no more than seven. If a company uses a value of seven, this variable will have a major impact on the number of levels of management in the firm.

Consider the problem of a company that wants to link design engineering more closely with production. A manager first decides that there is a need for a linking mechanism. That linking mechanism is best thought of as a design variable. The manager then considers what design alternatives exist for this variable. One idea is to place a production engineer in the design engineering group as the link between two organizations, although this alternative is expensive because it requires the use of an employee. A second idea is to establish a design coordination committee consisting of personnel from both the design and production groups; this committee might meet once or twice a month to go over new designs. A third idea is to use a technological solution: establish electronic mail links between the groups and encourage employees to use e-mail to better coordinate their efforts. If you are aiming for a T-Form organization, the third alternative might make the most sense for you.

Information Technology and Traditional Design Variables

Table 2.1 contains examples of key organization design variables that you can use to build an organization. It shows two types of variables: those that are traditional, or conventional (drawn from the literature on organization design), and those that involve information technology. Information technology is defined to include computers, videoconferencing, artificial intelligence, virtual reality, fax machines, cellular and wireless phones and pagers, all forms of electronic communication, and so on.

Conventional design literature typically fails to recognize the new design variables enabled by information technology. Yet, as in the example of the needed linking mechanism, such IT solutions as e-mail or groupware can often be used in place of such conventional solutions as task forces or liaison agents. These new IT-enabled variables may be totally distinct from traditional design variables, as we shall see when we examine virtual corporations. Or

Table 2.1. Traditional and IT Design Variables.

Class of Variable	Traditional Design Variables	IT Design Variables
Structural	Definition of organizational subunits	Virtual components
	Determining purpose, output of subunits	
	Reporting mechanisms	
	Linking mechanisms	Electronic linking
	Control mechanisms	
	Staffing	Technological leveling
Work process	Tasks	Production automation
	Workflows	Electronic workflows
	Dependencies	
	Output of process	
	Buffers	Virtual components
Communications	Formal channels	Electronic communications
	Informal communications/collaboration	Technological matrixing
Interorganizational relations	Make-or-buy decision	Electronic customer/supplier relationships
	Exchange of materials	Electronic customer/supplier relationships
	Communications mechanisms	Electronic linking

Source: Lucas and Baroudi, 1994, p. 14. Used by permission.

they may be an extension of a traditional variables, again as in the case of linking mechanisms.

Table 2.2 groups traditional and IT design variables into the four design categories described above: structural, work process, communications, and interorganizational relations. The IT design variables are discussed in more detail below.

Structural IT Design Variables

Virtual components. An organization can use IT to create organizational unit components in other than conventional form. For example, when manufacturers want parts suppliers to substitute for on-site inventory, the supplier is linked through electronic data interchange with the manufacturer; using overnight delivery, it provides parts to the manufacturer just as they are needed for production. The manufacturer now has a virtual raw materials inventory, which is owned by the supplier until it arrives for production.

Electronic linking. Through electronic mail, electronic or videoconferencing, and fax messages, it is possible to form links within and across all organizational boundaries. New workgroups can be formed quickly and easily.

Technological leveling. Technological leveling is the action of substituting IT for layers of management and for a number of management tasks. In some bureaucratic organizations, layers of management exist to look at, edit, and approve messages that flow from the level below them to the level above. With electronic communications, some of these layers can be eliminated. In addition, a manager's span of control can be increased since electronic communications can be more efficient than phone or personal contact for certain kinds of tasks, particularly those dealing with administrative matters.

Note that no single IT variable exists for the traditional variable of control mechanisms. Some firms use electronic information systems to provide control after an organization has been designed: system examples include budgets, project management applications, and similar monitoring systems. Chapter Seven describes how Mrs. Fields Cookies has used a variety of traditional and IT variables in creating an organization with extensive controls. However, even in that company, there is no one IT control variable in the design.

Work Process IT Design Variables

Production automation. The use of technology to automate manufacturing processes is well documented in popular magazines and newspapers as well as industry-specific publications. IT is also being used extensively for automating information-processing and assembly-line tasks in the financial industry. In cases where information is the product of a firm, IT is the factory. For white-collar workers, intelligent agents that roam networks provide one type of automation.

Electronic workflows. Interest in process reengineering has led to the development of workflow languages and systems. As organizations eliminate paper and perform most of their processing using electronic forms and images, workflow languages will be used to route documents electronically to individuals and workgroups that need access to them. Agents that can traverse networks to find information and carry messages will facilitate electronic workflows.

Communications IT Design Variables

Electronic communications. Electronic mail systems, electronic bulletin boards, and fax machines all offer alternatives to formal channels of communications.

Technological matrixing. Through the use of electronic communications, matrix organizations can be created at will. For example, a company preparing for a trade show could form a temporary task force from its marketing, sales, and production functions, using e-mail and groupware. Participants would report electronically to their departmental supervisors and to the team leader for the show, forming a matrix organization based on technology.

Interorganizational Relations IT Design Variables

Electronic customer/supplier relationships. Companies and industries are rapidly adopting electronic data interchange (EDI) and other forms of electronic communications to speed the ordering process and improve accuracy.

Examples of Designs Using IT Variables

It is possible to characterize four new organization structures that make use of the variables just described: virtual organizations, negotiated organizations, traditional organizations, and vertically integrated conglomerates. These prototypical organizations show a mixture of conventional and IT design variables and suggest some of the rich organizational forms that will appear in the future. They all can be viewed as precursors to the T-Form organization.

Table 2.2 summarizes the IT design variables that contribute to each organization's development. In some cases, the IT variable is substituted for traditional elements; in other cases, it is necessary for the very existence of an organizational form. In certain instances, the IT variable is optional or not applicable.

Virtual Organizations

Conventional organizations historically have grouped workers together for purposes of communications and coordination. In contrast to this physical nearness, IT design variables allow for virtual organizations. The virtual organization had its beginning fifteen to twenty years ago as people began to see the possibilities of using technology for work at home. With electronic communications capabilities, it is not clear that a physical organization is needed for many kinds of tasks.

For almost any organization that does not turn out a physical, durable product, one possible structural form is an amalgamation of independent agents. Today, for example, many catalog operations use individuals working from their homes using special telephones connected to an 800-number.

Cruiser, an experimental system at Bell Communications Research, uses small video cameras, a central computer, and a window on a computer screen to allow users to visit colleagues' offices without leaving their desks. This system could easily be extended to satellite offices and homes. Later, I discuss a commercial product that offers similar but less elaborate video features. In the more distant future, it is entirely possible that the notion of an office will disappear; consider, for example, the scenario for the Worldwide Group in Chapter One.

Table 2.2. Use of IT Design Variables
in Four Prototypical Organizations.

Organization Design Variable	Virtual Organizations	Negotiated Organizations	Traditional Organizations	Vertically Integrated Conglomerates
Virtual components	Substituted for physical components	Substituted for physical components	Used to replace isolated components	Forced onto electronic subsidiary
Electronic linking and communiations	Essential part	Essential part	Optional	Essential part
Technological matrixing	Used for everyone	Used for coordination	Used for various groups	Used for coordination and task forces
Technological leveling	Used to supervise remote workers and groups	NA	Used to reduce layers of management	Used to reduce layers of management
Electronic workflows	Used as crucial part of strategy	Used as crucial part of strategy	Used where applicable to restructure work	Become key to coordinating work units
Production automation	NA	Designs communicated	Used where applicable	Production coordinated among work units
Electronic customer/ supplier links	Used extensively	Used extensively	Becomes potentially important	Becomes key to operations

Source: Lucas and Baroudi, 1994, p. 16. Used by permission.

The virtual organization creates new management and coordination challenges. Some kind of virtual office may be necessary to assuage a manager's misgivings about supervision. Perhaps all members of a virtual organization like Worldwide will log in to virtual offices each morning to report in and have an electronic discussion with a supervisor.

At first, only technology companies like IBM and AT&T eliminated employee offices. AT&T has found that the reduced commuting resulting from the use of home offices allows its salesforce to spend 15 to 20 percent more time with customers. Now other firms are following suit. Chiat-Day, an advertising firm, has eliminated physical offices for a large number of employees. Compaq Computer Corporation moved its salesforce into home offices; sales and administrative expenses went from 22 percent of revenue to 12 percent, partially due to this change. Perkin-Elmer, a scientific equipment manufacturer in Connecticut, based 300 sales and customer service representatives in their homes, a move that allowed the firm to close thirty-five branch offices. (Some employees, however, have objected to losing their offices and to the expenses they incur for a home office.)

Negotiated Organizations

A second kind of IT-enabled organization is the negotiated organization. The California flower company Calyx & Corolla is based on two negotiated agreements. The first is with Federal Express to deliver flowers overnight to any destination in the United States at a favorable rate. The second agreement is with flower growers; instead of selling exclusively to wholesalers, the growers agree to put together a number of standard flower arrangements themselves. The final part of the organization is an 800-number and clerks who take orders. The orders are then sent via phone or fax to growers who prepare and address the arrangements for pick up and delivery by Federal Express.

Through these negotiated agreements and communications technology, this new company feels it can compete with the neighborhood florist and FTD. Calyx & Corolla is a negotiated organization in that its existence and profitability depend on the agreements it has with others and the service supplied to its customers by others. It is, in effect, a broker, using IT to coordinate its negotiated production facility and its negotiated delivery system (see also Chapter Seven).

An alliance that creates virtual components creates an ongoing interdependence between the two partners. The management challenge for the negotiated organization is to maintain service and quality. The firm depends on its partners to provide a product or service and yet has limited direct supervision of the business. Meeting service targets and deadlines and assuring adequate quality control can be difficult, although there are some methods that can be used. For example, the floral firm might place random orders with its growers to have flowers sent to its own management to test delivery time and product quality. Just as department stores have used unidentified shoppers for years to test their own personnel and service and to check on competition, the negotiated organization will need equivalent unidentified electronic shoppers.

Traditional Organizations

The two types of organizations just described are quite different from traditional corporations. Today, traditional organizations are also using technology to make some changes in structure but without making major modifications to the entire organization. An electronics manufacturer that sets up a just-in-time EDI link with a parts supplier, changing just one component of the organization, may still be primarily a traditional organization.

The traditional organization may call its redesign efforts reengineering. Merrill Lynch, for example, has completely reengineered the way it processes physical securities turned over to it by customers. This redesign has resulted in the closing of two processing centers and the creation of one new processing site. The firm has adopted image processing to dramatically reduce the need to physically handle securities, and the total number of individuals employed in handling securities has been cut by 50 percent (see also Chapter Six).

There are many other examples of the use of IT design variables to make changes in parts of traditional organizations; however, one enduring management challenge is to transform the traditional organization enough that it can take advantage of the cost savings and competitive opportunities made possible by technology.

The traditional organization needs to move toward the virtual model and toward the T-Form to improve its responsiveness. Today's business environment is characterized by rapid changes; slow-moving companies are at a major disadvantage. At a minimum, the traditional organization needs to take advantage of technological leveling to reduce layers of management, electronic matrixing to improve coordination, and electronic workflows to reduce paper handling.

The traditional organization today is at risk. IBM, one of the largest and most admired blue-chip companies in the 1960s and 1970s, is struggling with declining market share and bureaucracies that resist the kinds of sweeping change needed to be competitive. IT organization design variables can help managers restructure traditional organizations, making them more flexible. However, bringing about the changes that are possible given the technology is a formidable management task for which the staff of the traditional organization is not well suited.

Vertically Integrated Conglomerates

The last IT-enabled organizational prototype is the vertically integrated conglomerate, a form viewed by many of us with mixed emotions. The movement toward greater electronic exchange of data between customers and suppliers may be creating cases of vertically integrated conglomerates. The tendency for this form to emerge will be greater where there is a large power imbalance between the customer and the supplier.

As an example, General Motors requires virtually all of its suppliers to use electronic data interchange. For some suppliers, GM accounts for such a large proportion of their business that the supplier virtually becomes a component of GM, responding to its orders and demands. GM sends orders to the supplier's production scheduling system and is permitted to modify production schedules, priorities, and the like. The supplier has become a part of the large vertically integrated electronic conglomerate that exists around GM. Especially in relation to the small supplier, GM has thus obtained a substantial amount of control for little or no investment. GM can sever the relationship at any time at almost no cost to itself.

It is not clear that vertically integrated conglomerates are a desirable model for many organizations. Therefore, managers must be careful when establishing electronic links. They are very appealing from an efficiency standpoint; however, they can lock a firm into a relationship that reduces its independence. To the extent that the links are standardized (using, for example, an industry standard or an ANSI X.12 EDI protocol), the firms involved will have some flexibility in switching business relationships. If a link goes beyond simple exchange transactions and actually gives a customer access to the supplier's production planning systems, then the supplier risks becoming a part of a vertically integrated conglomerate, for better or for worse.

Adding People to the Design

One reaction to the discussion so far may be that it is a bit sterile. Where are the people? When do we consider how individuals relate to one another, how they are rewarded, and the nature of the tasks they perform? Where are organizational politics? For the most part, concerns about politics and emotions in organizations are not of unusual concern in the T-Form organization; they are no different in T-Form than in conventional organizations! Politics and the beliefs of senior managers are likely to determine the direction of the firm, its strategy, and how resources are allocated. The T-Form aspect of design remains neutral; its focus is on creating an efficient and competitive organization given the goals of senior managers.

People and tasks are an important component of any organization. A version of a classical model of organizations developed many years ago by Hal Leavitt suggests the interrelationships (Figure 2.1). As this model and some of the examples just described suggest, it may be difficult to change an organization if one attempts to alter only its structure, instead, managing people and tasks may create the greatest challenge for the organization designer.

Table 2.3 adds issues concerning people and tasks to those concerning structure and technology, in order to broaden our picture of organization design. The first three organizations in the table are conventional and have typical assumptions about people and task structures.

In a rigidly hierarchical organization, tasks are separated and decision making tends to be highly routinized. Tasks are defined by rules and practice, and risk is avoided. Bureaucracies assume that employees need to be motivated; they provide elaborate standards and procedures to tell each person how to do a job. A professional services firm is based on trust and professional conduct: for example, members of law and consulting firms tend to define their own tasks.

Figure 2.1. A Version of the Leavitt Model.

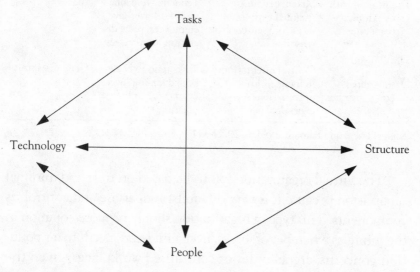

Source: Adapted from Lucas and Baroudi, 1994, p. 11.

Table 2.3. Additional Design Variables.

Structure and Technology (Grouping, Tasks, Jobs, Linkages)	People (Assumptions About Motivation)	Tasks (Especially Decision Making)	Example
Rigid hierarchy	People need external motivation.	No delegation; tasks designed for employee.	Military organizations
Bureaucracy	People want direction and procedures, are not good decision makers.	Limited delegation and decision authority.	Government; university (administration)
Adhocracy	People are professionals and can be trusted.	Loosely defined: individual decides how to best accomplish tasks.	Law firm; university (faculty)
Virtual	People can be trusted and self-control is assumed.	Distributed decision making.	Organization of the future?
Negotiated	Partners/alliances can be trusted.	Basic tasks defined in agreement; details left to individuals.	Calyx & Corolla
Traditional with electronic components	Mixed; people are regarded with some suspicion; self-control is assumed.	Tendency to define tasks for lower-level employees; some discretion for managers.	IBM
Vertically integrated conglomerates	Control orientation: individuals in linked organizations seen as expendable.	Tasks tend to be designed for employees, even those in linked organizations.	General Motors

Source: Lucas and Baroudi, 1994, p. 20. Used by permission.

The virtual organization has to be based on trust and minimal supervision because it is very difficult to supervise and control its components. This type of organization should be more common in the future as a number of forces, from child-care needs to air pollution concerns, argue for fewer centralized workplaces, given the commuting such a workplace necessitates.

In a negotiated organization, one must trust employees who are in allied companies. An agreement may specify the required output or level of service, but it will be up to each member of the alliance to accomplish its tasks as it sees fit.

The traditional firm with some electronic components tends to be large and will treat its employees in a variety of ways. There may be a tendency toward bureaucracy and toward defining tasks for lower-level employees. Technology can be used to distribute responsibility to lower-level managers or to centralize control over the organization; it all depends on the firm's assumption about employees and how it defines tasks, especially decision making.

The vertically integrated electronic conglomerate is very control oriented as it drives the systems of the different organizations to which it is linked; it avoids the need for, the expense, and the risks of traditional vertical integration. As a result, it tends to specify clearly how the firms connected to it electronically must operate.

People in the T-Form Organization

The pure T-Form organization will operate with the assumptions about people found in the virtual and negotiated organizations; managers will base supervision on trust in employees and on employees' self-control. Because it will not be possible to exert close physical supervision, the details of task definition and execution will be left up to the employee. Decision making will be moved to the lowest level of the organization where people have the information and knowledge to make the decision. Managers also have to trust partners in business alliances, since each partner depends on the other. People and tasks are an extremely important component of the T-Form organization.

Adopting the T-Form: An Example

An example illustrates how IT variables can be applied to the design of an organization. Assume that a traditionally structured manufacturer of electronic components wishes to take advantage of new technology to become a T-Form organization. ABZ is an actual company whose name has been changed to protect the innocent and the guilty (this manufacturer will be used as an example in several chapters).

Currently, ABZ has a very traditional organization structure; it has a headquarters with a small staff and a number of manufacturing plants in the United States and abroad. The largest of these plants is responsible for most information technology in the company. The firm has generally underinvested in technology and is behind its competitors in the industry. Fortunately for ABZ, its products are of high quality, and the company has not needed to compete on information technology.

Suppose that management has heard about the T-Form organization and would like to adopt it. What could this company do? (Table 2.4 summarizes how management at ABZ could use the IT design variables discussed in this chapter to restructure itself.) ABZ is currently being forced into becoming a *virtual supplier* by its customers who are moving to just-in-time production. It needs to develop the capability to query and monitor its customers' production control and scheduling systems so that it can send products as they are needed and so that the customer does not have to go through an ordering process.

IT can alter ABZ's reporting mechanisms as well. *Electronic communications* and groupware could reduce the amount of travel needed, especially between headquarters and the plants. *Electronic linking* could be used to link production planning, order entry, and marketing. The salesforce does not need individual offices; representatives could use notebook computers and home offices and concentrate on working with customers without the distractions of commuting and central office activities. Control could be enhanced by developing information systems that make control information available to various levels of management.

Technological leveling could be accomplished by reducing layers of management and providing communications tools like electronic

Table 2.4. An Example of IT Design.

Class of Variable	Conventional Design Variable	IT Design Variable	Applied to ABZ
Structural	Definition of organizational subunits	Virtual components	Manage virtual inventory for distributors; connect with customer production systems for JIT; use a common order entry system for a single point of contact; contract with overnight carrier for all distribution.
	Determining purpose, output of subunits Reporting mechanisms		Use more electronic communications to flatten structure; increase span of control.
	Linking mechanisms	Electronic linking	Link production planning, order entry, and marketing; use notebook computers for salesforce; eliminate private offices for salesforce.
	Control mechanisms		Develop systems to make control information more widely available.
	Staffing	Technological leveling	Reduce the number of layers in the organization by substituting electronic communications and groupware.
Work process	Tasks	Production automation	Continue efforts at automation.
	Workflows	Electronic workflows	Move toward total electronic tracking of order; use bar codes along with an electronic traveler to coordinate production.
	Dependencies		Coordinate with e-mail and groupware.
	Output of process		
	Buffers	Virtual components	
Communications	Formal channels	Electronic communications	Use e-mail and groupware, especially to communicate among distributed plants and headquarters.

Table 2.4. An Example of IT Design, Cont'd.

Class of Variable	Conventional Design Variable	IT Design Variable	Applied to ABZ
	Informal communications/collaboration	Technological matrixing	Use e-mail and groupware to coordinate on production forecasts and special projects.
Interorganizational relations	Make-or-buy decision	Electronic customer/ supplier relationships	Develop a home page on the Internet containing product information; as soon as feasible, use it or a commercial on-line service to allow customers to inquire on availability; other options are EDI and groupware.
	Exchange of materials	Electronic customer/ supplier relationships	(Same as above.)
	Communications mechanisms	Electronic linking	Establish e-mail links with customers; consider commercial services, EDI, and/or groupware.

mail and groupware to managers. ABZ has a large number of administrative support staff members and others not involved in direct production in the factories. This support organization adds overhead and is an excellent candidate for leveling.

In the factory, the company has been successful at moving toward *production automation*. Expanded efforts should focus on the creation of an electronic manufacturing environment. Orders would arrive electronically from customers; each order would generate a bar code to describe the customer and product. When production begins, a worker would attach a bar code to the physical tray that holds the product throughout the production cycle. At each stage, a worker at a workstation would use a wand to read the bar code, bringing up a screen with instructions on what operation to perform. At the end of production, after quality testing, the only paper necessary would be a label for the shipper.

Using electronic mail and groupware for *technological matrixing* and addressing the informal communications that are vital in managing a company, ABZ could quickly form task forces and other informal groups to solve problems. This approach would be particularly valuable for communications among plants. For example, one U.S. plant sends "kits" of product to be completed to a plant in Mexico. Various problems between the plants could be resolved quickly by using electronic communications rather than physical travel.

Technological matrixing would also facilitate a reduction in ABZ's managerial levels because it encourages employees to take the initiative in solving problems. Suppose that a customer contacts a marketing manager to ask if it would be possible to access ABZ's production scheduling system to schedule products to be built for the customer. The marketing manager, using e-mail and groupware, could form a task force in a matter of minutes, including personnel from production planning, marketing, information systems, and other interested areas. There should be no need to pass this request through layers of management in different departments. The task force could address the issue immediately and might never have to meet physically to develop a response for the customer.

ABZ needs to connect electronically to customers to provide them with a *virtual inventory*. It could also take advantage of more extensive *electronic customer/supplier relationships*. For example, ABZ could put up a home page on the Internet (see Chapter Eleven) or use a commercial on-line service like America Online or CompuServe to describe its products. As these services develop, ABZ could include information on the availability of various products as well. Another option would be to use groupware to exchange data electronically with customers and suppliers. Regular EDI and commercial e-mail services are available today to provide this kind of communication.

What will be the result of ABZ's adoption of IT design variables? Extensive use of electronic linking and communications will result in fewer layers of management, flattening the structure of the organization. Fewer organizational levels combined with the availability of information at all levels will push decision making down to lower levels of management. Easy electronic communications will encourage employees to contact appropriate colleagues to solve a problem rather than referring it up the hierarchy through a supervisor. Employees will be able to take on more responsibility because the structure of the organization will demand it and there will be an IT infrastructure to support them.

Some employees at ABZ will no longer have offices, especially the salesforce. ABZ will move toward complete electronic integration with customers and suppliers. Electronic mail for informal communications, EDI for routine transactions, and in some cases, direct links into customer information systems will increase the firm's responsiveness to customers and suppliers. *Electronic workflows* in production will eliminate paper, but more important, they will provide better service; production lots will not get lost if they are tracked electronically, and production workers will have accurate information on what tasks to perform for each order.

To accomplish this restructuring will take ABZ a long time since it has not kept up to date with technology. It will have to invest in a technological infrastructure and in people to develop the kind of IT applications described above. ABZ's product quality has helped it attain a commanding market share; adopting a T-Form organization would help it sustain its position and meet the threats of competitors who currently get more from their investment in IT than ABZ does.

Implications: The Challenge of Design

While each individual variable, each new use of technology, may sound like a small step, the overall impact of using IT design variables to create a T-Form organization will be profound. Instead of aging as it passes through channels or getting lost on someone's desk, information becomes a resource of the firm; it is processed and available instantaneously. The firm becomes a strategic partner with its suppliers and customers through electronic links and virtual components. Employees of the firm are finally empowered to solve problems themselves because they have the information and the ability to communicate easily with others who can help find a solution. Certainly the T-Form organization will be more efficient, but it also will be more effective in delivering a product or service compared to traditional organizations.

The major point of this chapter is that information technology has enabled new organization design variables and new types of organizations. Today's manager has many more options for designing an organization than his or her predecessor did even ten years ago. The problem today is that managers are faced in many instances with organizations that have existed for decades; these organizations typically have a traditional structure and do not change easily. It is not by accident that the most innovative forms of organization structure are shown by young start-up firms.

While it is easy to call for sweeping changes in our organizations, the reality of moving to these new forms is a different story. There have been occasional reports of success in reengineering, but these efforts have concentrated on only a small part of a firm's activities, such as the accounts payable section at Ford. How does one get an IBM, GM, or Digital Equipment Corporation to use IT to move toward becoming a T-Form organization?

There are few examples in the literature of massive change programs that have been successful. Kearns and Nadler (1992) have reported on their efforts to refocus Xerox Corporation on quality as the underlying focus of business. Their change program involved off-site seminars in which employees participated once as students and a second time as instructors. Despite this double exposure to the program, a number of employees still did not believe management was serious about the change. Kearns and Nadler do not present cost data, but the multiyear program they described represented a significant investment with considerable senior-level management support in refocusing the organization. The results were partially responsible for revitalizing a company that Kearns, on becoming chairman, was convinced might not survive.

Occasional departmental restructurings, for example, creating a single virtual workgroup, will not spread quickly enough to the rest of the organization to create significant structural changes. If a traditional organization wants to take advantage of the opportunities for new organizational forms offered by the IT design variables described here, it will have to undertake a massive change effort that is lead by senior management (Chapter Thirteen discusses this change process in more detail).

It is best when management recognizes the need for change before a crisis and devotes resources to restructuring the organization. The recent history of major firms that have experienced significant difficulties, however, shows that such early recognition is not usually the case. But managers have it in their power to change this pattern. Creating the changes required to take advantage of information technology design variables and to create a T-Form organization may be management's biggest challenge as we move into the twenty-first century.

Recommended Readings

Lucas, H. C., Jr., and Baroudi, J. "The Role of Information Technology in Organizational Design." *JMIS*, Spring 1994, pp. 9–23.

Nadler, D., and Tushman, M. *Strategic Organization Design*. New York: HarperCollins, 1988.

Chapter Three

Steps Toward Change: Preparation and Pitfalls

How does one prepare to design a T-Form organization? Table 3.1 presents six important actions for managers to take as they prepare to design or redesign an organization. This chapter discusses these actions and the potential benefits and pitfalls in using IT design variables.

Table 3.1. Actions to Prepare for Organization Design.

Preparation Action	Motivation
Develop a corporate strategy.	A strategy guides decisions about how to allocate resources and to structure the organization.
Understand the existing organization, its processes, and its systems.	Managers must understand what the organization does now in order to design a new structure for it.
Identify customers and markets.	Customer characteristics should influence the structure of the organization.
Analyze the industry.	Managers must identify both competitors and potential partners for forming alliances.
Develop an IT infrastructure.	Certain levels of technology must be in place before managers can succeed in building a T-Form organization.
Invest in and manage information technology.	Old technology becomes rigid; investment and continued management are required to retain flexibility.

Action 1. Chapter One discussed the importance of having a corporate strategy; this strategy needs to be in place before managers begin to design the T-Form organization. If a manufacturing company decides it wants to compete as the low-cost producer in its industry, it should undertake technology initiatives in production: for example, just-in-time inventory management systems with electronic links to suppliers. A manufacturing company that wants to compete primarily on customer service should probably focus on developing EDI links to customers. That is, the technology should be coordinated with strategy.

Action 2. Management must know the organization and its processes in order to redesign them. Many organizations have developed rigid departmental structures that focus on functions rather than on processes, such as order fulfillment. Instead of simply building separate information systems for manufacturing, finished goods inventory, and warehousing and shipping, managers in the T-Form organization will examine the entire process of shipping finished goods to customers. The resulting reengineered process may end up eliminating traditional functions; perhaps customers will be able to order electronically and schedule shipping directly from the factory as goods are completed. There will no longer be physical inventory or warehousing. Thus, understanding existing systems and processes is a prerequisite to an effective redesign of the organization using IT design variables.

Action 3. Many of the alternatives for an organization structure that relies on strategic grouping require that the firm know its customers and markets. The T-Form firm's electronic network is very likely to include markets and customers.

Action 4. Moreover, a firm needs to understand two other kinds of external organizations: competitors and potential partners in alliances. A firm is always influenced by its competition: will you beat your competitors to the T-Form and gain an advantage through IT design variables, or will you be catching up with companies that are well ahead? Knowing potential partners helps management decide where it makes the most sense to form an alliance rather than perform a task or process inside the firm.

Action 5. Chapter One outlined the infrastructure needed to develop the T-Form organization. Since technology requires a significant lead time to develop, a substantial portion of the IT infrastructure has to be in place before an organization can make much progress toward the T-Form.

Action 6. The organization also has to be able to manage the technology, something that has eluded a number of firms. (The chapters in Part Four discuss IT infrastructure in more detail.)

Some Potential Pitfalls in Design

Even with adequate preparation for organization design, there are still potential pitfalls. One of the biggest worries in using IT design variables is the possibility of creating technological rigidity instead of organizational flexibility. As we approach the twenty-first century, it is clear that organizations need to be flexible, which is not a characteristic many of us associate with technology. One challenge for us is to design an organization based on technology without a loss in flexibility. IT design variables are supposed to improve the organization; rigid technology will only make things worse.

How is the potential for technology to create rigidity best avoided? Much of the rest of this chapter is devoted to answering this question. The first answer is for managers to be sure that the technology they choose is as flexible as possible. Today, that means moving toward a client-server environment in which there is significant processing power on the user's desktop. Contemporary user workstations feature a broad range of programs that facilitate analysis of data and worldwide communications. These programs—spreadsheets, local database management systems, statistical packages, e-mail, groupware, and the like—let the user choose what kind of analyses to perform. He or she is not dependent on a programmer to create a custom application, a time-consuming process that decreases the user's flexibility.

A second answer to avoiding rigidity is to continue to invest in IT. Firms that tend to view technology as an expense rather than an investment often postpone modernizing their systems, but old systems are associated with rigidity, unfriendly user interfaces, and long delays in making changes. Firms that see technology as crucial to their business view IT as an investment. I recently visited the fixed-income trading floor of a major brokerage firm that had bought over 100 Sun workstations for its traders and developed a major new system for them. No one questioned the need for this investment.

The Flexible Organization

While flexible technology is vital, there is more to the organization than technology. In general, overall organizational flexibility can be defined as *the ability to adapt when confronted with new circumstances; a flexible organization defends quickly against threats and moves rapidly to take advantage of opportunities. It has the ability to adapt to change and respond quickly to market forces and uncertainty in its environment.* On another level, a quick response can mean different things to different people. If your competitor comes up with a new product or service, you need a quick response to adapt and avoid losing market share. Can you develop a new product and get it to the market quickly? Can you respond to a customer who demands a new kind of service? In manufacturing, a quick response may mean that you can switch quickly from making one product to another. For firms operating in a highly uncertain environment, flexibility means the firm adapts to the changes brought on by uncertainty.

IT Impact on Flexibility

Figure 3.1 illustrates the two ways in which information technology may affect organizational flexibility, increasing it or decreasing

**Figure 3.1. Information Technology and
Organizational Flexibility Model.**

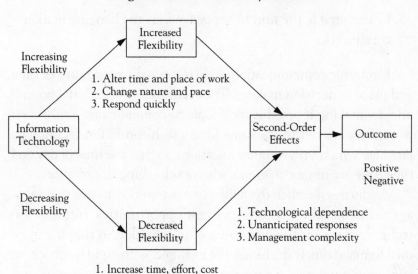

Source: Lucas and Olson, 1994, p. 158. Reprinted with permission from Ablex
Publishing Corporation.

it, with specific results in each case. The figure has two paths leading from the box labeled "Information Technology." The upper
path moves toward increased flexibility, while the lower path indicates the possibility for decreased flexibility from IT. In either
case, technology also has some second-order effects. All these
effects influence whether the impact of IT on flexibility is positive
or negative.

Information technology can increase flexibility in three major
ways.

1. IT can alter the time and place of work, generally by loosening boundaries that limited *where* tasks can be accomplished
   and removing constraints on *when* tasks can be performed.

2. IT can affect the nature and pace of work; most often it *speeds up* the processing of information.

3. IT can enable the firm to *respond quickly* to changing market conditions.

Electronic communications help remove the constraints of time and place in decision making. They remove organizational boundaries by making it possible for people to communicate easily even when they are not in the same location. Information technology provides asynchronous communications, so that the time of day and time zone are not a constraint when exchanging information.

As discussed earlier, the ability to react quickly means that management can take advantage of new opportunities. Information technology speeds the processing of information so that it can be used to make timely decisions. For example, with rapid feedback on consumer purchases, a garment manufacturer can change its production mix to meet the current market. IT also makes it possible to reconfigure manufacturing lines quickly, through flexible manufacturing systems. IT is the "factory" for the many financial services in which speed and processing power are required to provide service to the customer.

The Flexibility Paradox

Many managers, however, experience highly *inflexible* technology. You may question how IT can have the impact described in the top half of Figure 3.1. The bottom line from the "Information Technology" box in that figure represents the flexibility paradox: while technology may help a firm become more flexible, any given system eventually becomes old and inflexible compared to newer systems. In 1990, one insurance company was using an on-line system from 1967 that included a proprietary operating system! Imagine what would be involved to make changes to that application.

IT can create an unintended decrease in flexibility in two ways.

1. IT can increase the time, effort, and cost to change systems.
2. IT can increase the time, effort, and cost to change workflows and organization structure.

Systems undergo constant change and development; organizations spend 50 percent or more of their discretionary development dollars working on current as opposed to new systems. This kind of investment is necessary to adapt to new requirements and changing business conditions. If you fail to maintain and enhance old systems, your organization is left with rigid technology: you can then expect to face the negative side of the flexibility paradox. Your competitors will use technology to become more flexible while you struggle with inflexible technology that constrains rather than expands your options. Even though a particular application of technology may have started thirty years ago, your firm should not be executing that application with the same computer code, file structures, and output displays that were developed for the original system. Airline reservations systems have been around since the early 1960s; they still, at their core, are primarily intended to allow users to make reservations. However, these systems have been expanded, modified, and updated so many times that it is highly doubtful any of their original program code still exists. The price of flexibility is continued investment in technology to develop new applications and constantly update older ones.

Second-Order Outcomes from IT

Success in building technology for the flexible organization may also lead to three second-order outcomes, as can inflexible technology.

1. The organization can become more dependent on information technology than it was previously.

2. The use of IT may stimulate unanticipated responses from competitors, customers, the government, and other affected individuals or groups.

3. The organization may be faced with greater complexity, which has to be managed.

There is no question that most organizations have become more dependent on technology or that the T-Form will increase this dependence. It has been estimated that from 30 to 50 percent of capital investment in the United States is for information technology and that one in three U.S. workers uses a computer in some way. We shall see many examples in the following chapters of firms that could literally not function without technology. Airlines, for example, can not make reservations, assign seats, and load planes when their computers and communications networks are not operating properly.

You may also find that developing a new application raises major concerns from competitors or the government or some segment of the public. For example, a few years ago, Lotus Development Corporation created Lotus Marketplace Households, a marketing database on CD-ROM. However, various groups concerned with privacy decided that the product could be misused by companies who bought it. After information about the product was posted to an Internet bulletin board, Lotus chairman Jim Manzi received 30,000 electronic mail messages opposing the product. Lotus canceled the project.

After the 1987 stock market crash, several customers threatened to take their business away from brokerage firms that engaged in program trading. In program trading, the trader uses a computer program that spots discrepancies between stock and futures prices and automatically executes orders to take advantage of these differences. Some individuals thought that program trading contributed to the 1987 crash and decided to penalize firms that engaged in it.

Finally, as systems and communications networks are added to an organization, they create more complexity in that organization. Technology and complexity have to be managed, and many firms have encountered trouble when managers failed to take control of the organization's technology. More than anything else, management's willingness to lead the technology effort is what appears to separate the companies that gain flexibility with IT from those that lose it.

IT and Flexibility at the Airlines

The experiences of two industries demonstrate both how the overall effect of information technology can be increased flexibility and how second-order effects can crop up.

The first example is the airlines industry, which has a long history of using IT for all aspects of its operations. American Airline's computerized reservations system, SABRE, is one of the most famous IT applications. Realizing that its manual reservations procedures would break down with the advent of jet travel, American developed the SABRE system in the late 1950s in partnership with IBM.

SABRE was implemented in 1962, ahead of schedule, though it is rumored to have experienced significant cost overruns. The system removed the boundaries inherent in a manual reservations process. Each ticket agent had instantaneous access to an up-to-date centralized database of airline seats. A passenger with a telephone could make a reservation from almost any location at any time of the day or night, and the system thus created more flexibility for the airline and for its passengers.

During the late 1960s and early 1970s, the airline industry, concerned about pending deregulation, held talks about developing an all-industry reservations system that could be deployed in travel agencies. This attempt at a single system failed, and United Airlines and American both began to place their reservations terminals in travel agencies (see Chapter Four).

Throughout the thirty-plus years American Airlines has had a computerized reservations system (CRS), it has illustrated how firms need to stay up to date with technology if they want to enjoy the flexibility it offers. Probably the most difficult decision for the airline occurred in the early 1960s, when IBM brought out its third generation of mainframe computers.

American developed SABRE on second-generation machines that had been specially modified to run the on-line reservations application. There was no easy way to convert the second-generation code to newer computers, yet the airline knew that it would need their capacity as the system grew.

Based on its experience of developing SABRE with American Airlines, IBM created a new airline reservations package, called PARS (Passenger Airline Reservations System), that ran on its new, third-generation computers. Eastern Airlines bought PARS and began to customize the package for its own environment. American ended up purchasing the Eastern version of PARS and turning it into the base for its next generation SABRE system, a fact that was not widely publicized at the time. At this point, Eastern probably had the technological lead in reservations systems, but it was "outmanaged" by American and United, which moved aggressively to place reservations terminals in travel agencies.

American and United (joined by several other carriers) expanded their travel agency business rapidly. They added new features to make the systems easier to use and to encourage agents to take advantage of them. One useful application was the module that allows travel agents to print boarding passes to be included with tickets. Without a boarding pass, the traveler must stand in line for a seat assignment and pass. The CRS, working through the travel agent, moved part of the process of boarding the aircraft out of the airport and into the agent's office. In this way, the system altered the boundaries of the airport and speeded up the boarding process for passengers.

The automation of travel agencies was also a great boon to agency business; before agency CRSs, travel agents made a minority of ticket sales. Today, it has been estimated that agents generate 70 to 80 percent of ticket sales. CRS deployment in travel agencies has changed the nature of the travel business.

Another benefit of the CRS has accrued to the airlines—the wealth of data they have on their own operations and on passengers' plans. With a database of all reservations, an airline can practice "yield management." An airline computer contains a profile of each flight, showing the expected sales of seats in each class by a given day before the flight is to depart. For example, historically there may have been twenty full-fare coach seats sold fifteen days before a specific flight. If the yield management program sees that demand for full-fare seats is higher—say, twenty-five—it might alert a pricing specialist who, in turn, could reduce the number of discount seats available so more full-fare seats could be sold. Yield management has allowed the airlines to generate significant additional revenue from their flights.

Over the past thirty years, airline CRSs have had four significant impacts.

1. They provide better customer service. Travel agents can be more responsive; passengers with access to a network service like CompuServe or Prodigy, can access an easy-to-use version of SABRE, called EAASY SABRE, from their personal computers.

2. The systems have generated revenue. When an airline makes a reservation for another carrier on its reservations system, the CRS vendor charges a ticket fee (currently in the neighborhood of $2 to $3) for each leg of the flight. American and United have highly profitable CRS subsidiaries whose revenues come from these ticketing fees.

3. The systems have created barriers to entry. It would be very difficult to start an airline without access to a CRS; not having one's flights listed in travel agency computers would make it difficult to sell tickets. In this sense, the CRSs have created less flexibility for new entrants while they have increased the flexibility (and power) of existing CRS vendors.

4. The structure of the industry has changed; as mentioned above, the major system vendors now own CRS subsidiaries. There are also alliances of European airlines to build reservations systems as a defensive move to keep American Airlines from capturing all the travel agents abroad.

Their reservations systems have also created some second-order problems for the airlines. The Department of Transportation has issued regulations to try to prevent abuse of the systems (see Chapter Four). Bills have been brought before Congress—none passed into law or active now—that would force CRS vendors to divest themselves of their subsidiaries that operate the systems. Also, the airlines have become very dependent on technology. Even American has had occasional maintenance problems arising from technological complexity. In one instance, a runaway program erased critical indices that pointed to reservations, and caused the CRS to crash; the resulting outage lasted more than twenty-four hours. At another time, American actually reduced its quarterly profits by an estimated $50 million because it accidentally closed some flights to discount fares when those flights had seats available. Given their critical dependence on technology, the airlines have to maintain a high level of competence in managing IT.

IT and Flexibility in the Securities Industry

The securities industry provides another example of the organizational flexibility that IT can provide. The brokerage industry first used technology simply to process large volumes of daily transactions. A brokerage firm must keep track of all its customers' accounts while the stock exchanges and clearing firms must settle all of the day's transactions. In the 1960s, the stock exchanges closed early to give firms time to catch up with processing; today, transaction volumes much higher than those of the 1960s are handled routinely by elaborate computer systems. IT has provided the securities industry with the flexibility to keep up with this huge volume of transactions and even to speed up the processing of customer trades and records. During the week of October 19, 1987, for example, the New York Stock Exchange handled more volume than it had during an entire year a decade earlier!

In addition, what was once "back office" information on customers' holdings is now available on-line to each broker, and he or she can now serve a customer much better than in the past. The ability to process large amounts of data quickly has also made new financial instruments possible, and thus IT has also given brokerage firms the ability to market new products and services to existing customers. Many "derivative" instruments—that is, financial instruments based on some other security (for example, mortgage-backed securities)—need computer processing to exist. And as mentioned, the technology also makes possible strategies like program trading. It would be very difficult to monitor the information necessary to make a program trade and very difficult to execute the trade without the speed and processing ability of a computer and communications network.

Once all the needed data are available from one's workstation, is it necessary to meet and have a physical exchange for a trade to take place? The existing regional exchanges, the New York Stock Exchange and the American Stock Exchange, can explain in great detail why one needs a physical market and a specialist system. NASDAQ (National Association of Securities Dealers Automated Quotations) disagrees; this stock exchange does not exist in a single physical location. Rather, it is a computer network; the participants in the exchange use computer terminals and can be located anyplace that has communications capabilities with the NASDAQ network. In addition, Reuters has an electronic network that handles about 30 percent of the world's foreign exchange transactions. Other electronic networks, like the Instinet and the Arizona Stock Exchange, follow a variety of auction procedures. These electronic marketplaces are virtual exchanges: they appear to exist in some traditional ways, but in reality, they have a much different form than we are used to.

The physical exchanges are now adding technology to compete with electronic networks. The SuperDot system at the New York Stock Exchange routes orders directly to specialists, avoiding the floor broker. This system helps the small investor obtain service and can handle trades up to 30,000 shares or limit orders of 99,999 shares.

The overall possible impact of all this information technology on the securities industry falls into three areas.

1.   Better customer service: brokers have more information and can provide better advice and trade execution for customers. A number of discount brokerage and mutual funds firms now provide PC software that allows individual investors to enter their own trades. Currently, the brokerage firm has to execute the trades, but in the future, there will be no technological reason why these trades could not go directly to an exchange.

2.   Possible increased market volatility: during the crash of 1987, one mutual fund company sold $1.7 billion in assets while three other firms sold over $800 million each because they needed cash for customer redemptions. It may be that the technology that allows the management of huge mutual funds has created an unstable market.

3.   Possible discouragement of individual investing: it has been suggested that individual traders may feel they can never get a fair deal in their personal trading given the sophistication of the technology available to large firms.

IT has provided the securities industry with more flexibility, but that flexibility has many effects. Technology has created extensive competition for the existing physical exchanges. It is now possible to conduct twenty-four-hour-hour trading by passing "the book" around the world from New York to London to Tokyo. And not all firms have successfully managed the technology; even some of the most well-known financial institutions have experienced expensive systems failures. The head of the London Stock Exchange resigned in 1993 over the failure of the Taurus settlements system, a project that had dragged on for twelve years and was still not finished.

In short, in both the airlines and securities industries, IT has had a significant impact on flexibility, but some firms have been far more successful than others in taking advantage of this flexibility for themselves and in passing the benefits on to customers. The airline reservations systems have been extremely profitable for their owners; simultaneously, customers have much more flexibility in dealing with airlines and in planning travel. Perhaps airlines have been among the front-runners in using IT because computer technology seems to fit the high-technology image of an airline, and the needed investment in computers probably does not seem so expensive when compared with the airlines' investments in aircraft. Technology also helps the securities industry manage its transactions and create and offer new products, many of which, in turn, are helpful to its customers.

Three Areas of Flexibility

The experience of the securities and airline industries also illustrates how information technology affects flexibility primarily in the three areas mentioned earlier.

Time and place. IT alters the time and place where a task can be accomplished. You can make an airline reservation twenty-four hours a day from anyplace that you can find a phone. You can trade securities twenty-four hours a day if you have a PC (though your trade will not be executed until the exchange opens for business). Brokers can be in touch with their databases when out of the office; airline managers can send electronic mail messages around the world to different time zones.

Nature and pace of work. Technology typically affects the nature and pace of work by speeding up information processing. Airlines now have huge (billions of characters) databases that allow them to do things like closely manage the revenue yield of each flight. IT enables the securities industry to process huge volume of trades each day and speeds up the settlement process.

Response time. Finally, information technology allows firms to take action promptly when some situation changes or is about to change. Yield management programs allow airlines to respond quickly to patterns of ticket sales. Databases and networks let brokers quickly monitor and target different customers. The physical exchanges are using technology to compete with the speed of virtual marketplaces created by technology. Brokerage firms using technology require very short lead times to create and market new products.

Implications

The examples from the airlines and the securities industries illustrate two aspects of technology other than increased flexibility that are also important for managers to consider if they are to avoid IT pitfalls: the management of IT and systems design.

First, airlines and securities firms *carefully chose what systems to develop*. Second, these companies *successfully implemented the chosen technology*. It was management that initiated the needed development projects, provided funding, and monitored progress. The systems described in this chapter were not developed solely by a systems analysts and programmers; management committed organizations and their resources to building systems that changed the way their industries did business.

As managers prepare for designing the T-Form organization, they must heed warnings about what can go wrong as well as anticipate the benefits of doing things right. Managers have to understand their firm's strategy and its operations in order to design or redesign the organization appropriately. Managers should also be familiar with their industry, customers, and markets. They must also take great care in developing and managing the technology they choose to use, so that it does not create a rigid organization. One of the greatest virtues of the T-Form organization is its high degree of flexibility; it would indeed be tragic if management instead produced a rigid, dysfunctional organization through a substantial investment in the wrong technology.

Recommended Reading

Lucas, H. C., Jr., and Olson, M. "The Impact of Information Technology on Organizational Flexibility." *Journal of Organizational Computing*, Jan. 1994, pp. 155–176.

Part Two

The Dramatic Impact of Information Technology

The first part of this book described how information technology might be used to create new organizational forms and how IT design variables can make it possible to design firms that will be able to compete in the next century. Part Two shows how technology has already had a significant impact on industries and firms and suggests ways that you can apply IT design variables to move toward a T-Form organization.

Chapter Four explores technology and competitive strategy, discussing how three companies used technology actively to pursue their competitive strategies. The results achieved by these firms should provide confidence that technology, when properly managed, can make a major contribution to an organization. The results show compelling reasons to use IT design variables to structure an organization.

Chapter Five describes the impact of technology on markets, a fundamental component of our economy. Technology assists companies in obtaining the information necessary to participate in a market and reduces purchasing cycle times. As firms today take advantage of technology to create and use electronic markets, it is time to consider even greater use of electronic customer/supplier links and of virtual organizational components.

Chapter Six visits reengineering, or business process redesign, one of today's most popular business topics. Business process redesign often involves applying IT design variables to a single process or part of an organization. This chapter can help you identify and modify processes, an important part of organization design. Examples of two companies that have reengineered their corporate structures suggest that one way to view the use of IT design variables is as a reengineering effort aimed at creating a T-Form organization.

Chapter Four

Corporate Strategy: Creating the New Road Map for Competing

This chapter focuses on the IT design variables of *electronic linking and communications, electronic customer/supplier relationships*, and *virtual components* as they are used by three companies to enable their competitive strategies.

Types of Corporate Strategies

A corporate strategy is a road map for competing. It consists of goals and a program for achieving them. In some firms, strategy is explicit and is discussed among employees; in others, strategy is implicit and must be deduced from the actions of the firm. The most important strategies are ones that focus on the competition; how do we obtain an advantage that lets us capture market share and/or greater profits?

As I have discussed, your strategy ought to have a large influence on how you structure your organization and on the kind of technology you build. If you want to be a low-cost producer, you are more likely to be interested in designing a corporation with a lot of virtual components in order to take advantage of other people's overhead. Conversely, I have seen companies with a strong marketing and sales emphasis hindered in achieving their objectives because they have applied technology only to their finance function.

Three Generic Strategies

Porter (1980) has identified three generic strategies that firms pursue:

1. Low-cost producer: the firm tries to have the lowest costs in the industry and compete on price.

2. Differentiation: the firm tries to differentiate itself from competitors and to create a demand for its products. According to BMW, for example, some people drive "cars" while others enjoy "ultimate driving machines." BMW has been very successful at differentiating its products from other automobiles.

3. Market niche focus: the firm finds a market niche and exploits it. Hermés has done very nicely by producing high-quality, expensive products for a relatively limited clientele.

In today's competitive economy, firms are tending to focus on more specific strategies than before. Most of the time, a firm adopts one of the generic strategies described by Porter, but it might be able to follow two at the same time.

Within these generic strategies, firms often have an additional focus. The *customer-driven* firm focuses on its customers: How can we provide better service? How can we design products that meet our customers' needs? What technology exists that will help us better serve customers? Customer service is extremely important in commodity businesses, for example, the mail-order sales of personal computers.

Each firm has a variety of cycle times; a typical one is the length of time it takes to design a new product or service. Therefore, a second important additional strategy is to *reduce cycle times*. Chrysler has been particularly successful in reducing the time it takes to design and to build a car, and automakers in general are moving toward parallel development, a strategy that requires new organization structures. Instead of designing a car's parts sequentially, a design team reduces cycle time by working on all parts of a new car project at the same time. This strategy also increases coordination among team members and allows problems to surface more quickly than they did in traditional, sequential development.

In the light of the increasing unification of Europe, some firms have decided to follow a strategy of *global competition* in the marketplace, as opposed to operating in local markets alone. ASEA Brown Boveri is an excellent example of a global company; national boundaries play a very small role in its decisions on where to manufacture or locate employees.

In the United States, the first part of the 1980s saw an economic boom, leading to a number of corporate excesses. The late 1980s and the early 1990s have been marked by economic downturns and slow growth. To compete in this difficult economy, firms have attempted to determine their "right" size. Usually, the strategy of *right-sizing* has meant a significant reduction in the number of workers in the firm and rather large write-offs for restructuring. Such blue-chip companies as IBM and DEC have reduced their levels of employment by tens of thousands of workers. To a large degree, right-sizing has mostly amounted to down-sizing.

Japanese manufacturers have gained a large market share in a number of industries partially through a fanatical *devotion to quality*. Now many firms around the world are focusing their strategies on quality in the hopes of getting ahead of the competition. Quality is an obvious concept in the manufacturing sector, but services firms are also learning to compete by focusing on the quality of their services.

There are many factors that contribute to a firm's achieving a competitive advantage as it follows its corporate strategy, and one of them is information technology. In the following sections, I describe several different firms and industries where the evidence is very strong that part of the competitive advantage these firms have gained while following the kinds of strategies outlined here has come from their use of information technology (see Table 4.1).

IT and Strategy at American Airlines

One of the most frequently cited examples of competitive advantage comes from the airlines industry. In the late 1950s, American Airlines, seeing the approach of jet travel, joined with IBM to develop its now famous SABRE reservations system, as discussed in

Table 4.1. Strategy and Technology Examples.

Company	Strategy	Role of Technology
American & United Airlines	Customer service through agency automation	Only way to provide ability for widespread flight reservations
Rosenbluth Travel	Customer service through value-added services	Provided incremental services built on airline reservations systems
Kennametal	Low-cost producer; customer service; tool management for customers	Redesigned entire IT effort; built links to customers

the last chapter. SABRE was soon joined by United Airlines's APOLLO system. Several other airlines attempted to develop their own systems with different mainframe computer vendors, but most ended up using IBM's Passenger Airline Reservations System (PARS) (this example draws upon Copeland and McKenney, 1988).

The decision of American Airlines to invest in SABRE was not a trivial one. Max Hopper, the American Airlines executive most associated with SABRE over its lifetime, told a seminar at New York University in 1992 that the company faced an initial investment in development costs of $40 million: "the figure was equivalent to the cost of four Boeing 707s, which was the largest plane flying in those days. And if we had bought aircraft instead, it would have been a 20 percent increase in the existing jet fleet. So, diverting our capital from jets to exotic technology, I think, was a very major commitment and a significant financial risk for us as a company."

American established itself as a technology leader among the airlines with its development of SABRE. Then, in 1976, an all-industry effort to develop a computerized reservations system (CRS) for travel agents broke down. The development was to be financed by the major carriers in relation to their size. Given its size, United Airlines felt it would bear an unfair burden compared to the benefits, and it pulled out of the consortium, announcing that it would install terminals connected to its own CRS in travel agencies. American soon followed suit, and the great travel agency automation battle was joined.

What does an airline gain by having its CRS in a travel agent's offices? In the early days of automation, those airlines without a presence in any agencies complained that the CRS vendors obtained an advantage through dirty tricks. For example, it was common for a CRS vendor to list its own flights first on the agent's screen. If you called an agent using SABRE and asked for flights from New York to Chicago, all of American's flights would appear first followed by the flights for other carriers. For a crowded market like the New York to Chicago route, American's flights would easily fill up the first display screen. Since agents make 90 percent or more of their reservations from the first screen, American would get more than its "fair share" of bookings.

By 1984, this "display bias" and other complaints, primarily against American and United, led the Department of Transportation (DOT) to issue a series of rules regulating computerized reservations systems, including, among others, the rule that "system vendors may not use criteria related to carrier identity in ranking and listing flights on a reservations display; the listing criteria must be consistently applied to all carriers, including the system vendor, and to all markets" (*Federal Register*, 1992, pp. 43780–43837).

CRS vendors did change the basis of their displays, but the smaller carriers have charged the dominant vendors with introducing subtle biases in their systems that discriminate against non-CRS vendors. For example, a CRS vendor could make it more difficult to complete a complicated transaction for another carrier than for one of its own flights. The DOT continues to revise and to regulate computerized airline reservations systems, even though much regulation of airlines themselves has been dropped.

Are there other ways the airlines might benefit from these

systems? My colleagues Rob Kauffman and Kathie Duliba and I have investigated a "halo effect" of agency automation, using an extensive set of data about airline performance and strategy (Duliba, Kauffman, and Lucas, 1994). This halo effect occurs when the travel agent, using, say, the United Airlines CRS, books more flights on United than are ordinarily expected. Suppose you then call a travel agency that uses United's APOLLO CRS. The agency's APOLLO terminal must display the available flights without bias, but suppose that the agent, due to his frequent contact with United, suggests United flights to you when you ask what is available. Under these conditions, the airline with its CRS in that travel agency's offices might end up with a higher than expected market share for that agency's city. This increased market share would be expected to show up in overall airline performance.

The data that we have collected and analyzed fits that scenario. During the period in which most travel agent automation was taking place, the dominant CRS vendors had higher than expected market share and had better performance than airlines that did not participate in agency automation.

The last way in which an airline benefits from placing its CRS in agents' offices is through direct commissions. The CRS vendor charges the airline for whom it makes a reservation $2 to $3 for each leg, or ticket, on a trip. While CRS vendors are criticized for this practice, their fee is considerably smaller than the charges that are added to theater tickets by automated vendors. Given the volume of air travel, these fees mount up quickly. American Airlines's SABRE subsidiary is the most profitable part of its business. In fact, when discussing legislative threats to force airlines to divest themselves of their CRS subsidiaries, Robert Crandall, American's chairman, was reported to have said that if forced to break up American, he might just sell the airline and keep the reservations system!

Clemons and Weber (1991) have identified five ways a firm might obtain a competitive advantage. It is interesting to see how the dominant airline CRS vendors have followed these strategies:

1. Be the first mover: the leading CRS vendors are the airlines who first developed reservations systems and first marketed them to travel agencies.

2. Maintain technological leadership: the airlines' computerized reservations systems feature some of the most advanced information technology found today.

3. Create high switching costs: through technology and legal agreements, the airlines have attempted to raise the costs of switching from one CRS to another for travel agents. Early agency contracts contained provisions for liquidated damages if the agency terminated a contract, and purchasing any new equipment extended the contract for five years!

4. Apply continuous innovation: following the initial rollout of dumb terminals, CRS vendors then gave agencies PCs with programs to automate the operations of the agencies themselves.

5. Invest your resources in technology: the major CRS vendors tend to be the largest airlines, those with more resources for buying and developing technology.

Given continuing regulation and a mature industry, we might expect that CRSs would be creating no controversy today. In early 1994, however, several major reservations systems decided to drop Southwest Air from their systems. This action meant that travel agents would not have easy access to Southwest schedules and fares.

Southwest has always refused to pay booking fees, but the CRS vendors list its schedules and fares as a convenience to their agents. (Southwest does pay SABRE for this listing, but it refuses to pay for ticketing. SABRE did not drop Southwest.) The action by several CRS vendors meant that travel agents were faced with writing Southwest tickets by hand, something many probably had forgotten how to do. In fact, one commentator expressed concern that there might not be enough ticket stock available for handwritten tickets!

It appeared that Southwest would be at a significant disadvantage if agents were forced to write tickets by hand, but shortly after the CRS vendors' announcements, Southwest said that it would offer a personal computer system to travel agents who sold at least fifteen Southwest tickets each day. The PC system features a ticket printer and a toll-free number for calling Southwest ticket agents. Southwest stated that it could not be a low-fare airline if it had to pay booking fees; it estimated that ticket fees for APOLLO alone, which is now owned by a group of eleven airlines, would cost it $30 million a year. CRSs still play a major competitive role in the airline industry.

IT has not only provided those airlines that took advantage of it with significant benefits, it has changed the nature of the travel industry. The major CRS vendors have large, profitable reservations subsidiaries, and travel agents, as mentioned earlier, now write about 70 to 80 percent of all tickets, compared to 40 percent or so prior to agency automation. The technology has also provided a very high level of customer service. It is doubtful that an airline could compete today without having access to and its schedules and fares available through some system that travel agents can access.

From the standpoint of IT design variables, airline reservation systems make extensive use of electronic linking, electronic communications, and electronic customer/supplier relationships. Airlines were among the first organizations to see the benefits these IT design variables could bring for improving customer service and efficiency.

IT and Strategy at Rosenbluth Travel

Even when they were beginning to develop their reservations systems, airlines were large organizations. They had or made resources available for technology. Can the small firm gain an advantage from IT? Eric Clemons and Michael Row (1991) have written about a small local travel agency that used IT to become a major nationwide player. Rosenbluth Travel, headquartered in Philadelphia, has grown from $40 million in sales in 1980 to $1.3 billion in 1990. It is now one of the five largest travel management companies in the United States and has over 400 offices.

Rosenbluth has been extremely effective in taking advantage of the opportunities offered by deregulation in the travel industry and in using technology to manage the complexity of modern travel and to obtain economies of scale. Rosenbluth invested in the necessary IT over a period of years. While the expenditure in any one year was not inordinate, Rosenbluth created a technology base that would be extremely difficult for a new entrant or even an existing competitor to match.

Prior to deregulation in 1976, the role of the agent was basically to make a reservation and distribute a ticket. Deregulation changed that role. Now the travel agent is expected to manage the increased complexity of travel for the traveler. American Airlines's SABRE system has contained up to forty-five million fares and processed forty million changes a month. The travel agent is expected to help his or her clients use this information, without a bias toward a particular airline. In addition, businesses have become very interested in managing their travel; it is the third largest expense for most firms after payroll and information services. Businesses have been working out negotiated rates with airlines, hotels, and rental car companies. Thus, in the era of airline deregulation, Rosenbluth's major business focus has been managing travel complexity, especially for the corporate travel market.

The following list of Rosenbluth's critical technology moves illustrates how the firm has used IT for adapting to current conditions and expanding its business:

1. Around 1981, Rosenbluth experimented with processing data from airline computerized reservations systems (CRS) to provide information for corporate accounts.

2. In 1983, Rosenbluth introduced READOUT, a program that listed flights by fare and thus made it possible to see the fare

implications of taking a particular flight. The normal flight display listed flights by departure time, and the agent had to move to another screen to obtain fare information.

3. In 1986, Rosenbluth developed VISION, a proprietary back-office system that produced highly flexible reports for clients. The system created a record of transactions made for a client at the time of ticketing no matter the location of the agency or the CRS in use. This system gave Rosenbluth independence from the data provided by the airline CRSs. Rosenbluth estimated that it invested nearly half of its pretax 1986 profit in VISION. The system produced reports about two months before agencies using only the airline CRS could. It was also more flexible than other agencies' CRS-dependent systems. Rosenbluth was able to negotiate special fares with the airlines on heavily traveled routes identified by VISION. Around this time, Rosenbluth also began a new pricing strategy. Instead of competing for corporate clients by offering to rebate part of its commission, Rosenbluth tried to change its relationship with clients to one of cooperation. It promised clients that it could reduce overall travel costs through lower fares, and it used VISION reports to document the savings.

4. In 1988, Rosenbluth used a new feature in United's APOLLO reservations system to support intelligent workstations. The new Rosenbluth system, PRECISION, made client and individual employee travel profiles and the READOUT database available to the agent making a reservation. ULTRAVISION, another Rosenbluth system that runs with the normal reservations process, monitors transactions for accuracy and completeness.

5. In the 1990 to 1991 time frame, Rosenbluth began installing USERVISION in customer offices. This system lets the user make flexible queries about corporate travel. The data are one day old compared to the forty-five-day lag typical of the airline CRS data.

These initiatives have been associated with the tremendous growth cited earlier to $1.3 billion in sales in 1990 and the increase in offices to over 400.

Rosenbluth's technology strategy has been to compete through value-added services rather than through being the low-cost producer and offering rebates. However, the company also meets jointly with its clients and service providers to help clients negotiate the lowest possible fares.

Rosenbluth has been extremely successful. And some of this success can be attributed to its investment in technology. The firm took risks in developing new uses of IT, and it developed in-house expertise to successfully implement systems. It also took advantage of IT design variables, especially electronic customer/supplier relationships with the airlines and electronic linking and communications with customers, to market new services to its clients. Business and technology strategies developed together in an integrated approach to growth.

IT and Strategy at Kennametal, Inc.

The examples so far have centered on service businesses, but information technology is also vital to manufacturing firms. Kennametal, Inc., located in Latrobe, Pennsylvania, is a leading producer of metalworking and mining tools. The company invested heavily in technology in the 1980s to counter foreign competitors and to try to reverse its loss of market share ("Kennametal Finds the Right Tools," 1992).

By 1991, Kennametal had moved into the ranks of the Fortune 500 and had achieved a net income of $21 million on sales of $618 million. It had also managed to fight off its major European competitor who was trying to gain market share in the United States; it even doubled its own European market share to 8 percent. Recently, it opened a $25 million R&D building near its headquarters.

Kennametal is focusing on customer service and reduced cycle times. The major thrust of its IT investment has been to serve customers more quickly and reduce inventories. For example, Kennametal will stock and manage tool storage areas for some customers.

What got Kennametal started? In 1978, a new president joined the firm. He came from the aerospace industry in California, and he felt Kennametal was a decade behind the times. Computers were used in accounting and almost nowhere else; Kennametal had an aging Honeywell mainframe and used punched cards for processing. As is often the case, the first efforts to turn the technology around failed, due to problems with an outside contractor and a lack of planning. However, management had the determination to persevere.

The IT project leader brought in several important customers to help plan a system that required three years to create. The new system lets Kennametal managers find out within seconds what tool products are available at different sites around the country. As a result of Kennametal's capabilities, GM's Saturn division chose it as the sole supplier of all metalcutting tooling.

Kennametal has also been very active in pursuing electronic data interchange (EDI). Orders from large customers like General Electric arrive electronically and are processed directly by Kennametal computers. A person does not get involved in the order until a picking list is sent to the warehouse and the items are actually chosen and packed for delivery to the customer. The company has also provided its North American salesforce with laptop computers for use in e-mail, sales reporting, record keeping, and inquiring about the availability of products.

Kennametal illustrates the use of electronic linking and communications with its own employees and electronic customer/supplier relationships through EDI. It also displays a virtual component: the tool inventories that it manages for customers. Kennametal is a partner in an alliance with customers to manage a component of their businesses. The customer depends on Kennametal for service, and Kennametal depends on the customer to provide it with information on what tools to stock and when to provide them.

Implications

The T-Form organization, like any firm, needs a strategy in order to compete. IT design variables help this organization implement its chosen strategy and, in fact, may suggest a strategy to the firm. IT design variables facilitate strategies for firms that want to be the low-cost producer or the high-quality provider, that want to reduce cycle times, emphasize customer service, become global organizations, and/or right-size themselves (see Table 4.2 for a summary of the IT design variables used by each company in this chapter). *Electronic linking and communications, electronic customer/supplier relationships, virtual components,* and the other IT design variables are an important part of developing and implementing strategy for the T-Form organization. Subsequent chapters will provide examples of other firms that have used technology in creative ways to achieve their competitive strategies.

What must you do to use information technology strategically? First, you must have a corporate strategy, and that strategy should be communicated to all employees. Second, you have to be willing to invest in technology to help achieve your objectives, just as

Table 4.2. IT Design Variables and Strategy.

IT Design Variable	Example
Electronic linking and communications	American and United CRSs; Rosenbluth, links with customers; Kennametal, links for internal operations
Electronic customer/supplier relationships	American and United CRSs, with travel agents and passengers; Kennametal, for tool management; Rosenbluth, with airlines
Virtual components	Kennametal, customer tool inventory

we saw American Airlines and Kennametal invest in IT and a technology infrastructure when there were many other options for scarce funds. Finally, you have to be able to manage the technology, which is the most formidable challenge managers face when it comes to IT.

After over two decades of teaching management students and executives, conducting research, and consulting with companies, I am convinced that the most significant problems we have with technology are managerial in nature. In fact, I suggest that if you believe that IT is only for technicians, you are inviting disaster. Yes, IT is different from other components of your business, but any manager can learn enough about IT to understand the ways that it can make a positive contribution to his or her firm. (I discuss some approaches to managing IT in the organization in Chapter Thirteen.)

In short, once again, to use technology successfully in designing the organization, you must have a strategy, a technology infrastructure, and confidence in your ability to manage IT.

Recommended Readings

Clemons, E., and Row, M. "Information Technologies at Rosenbluth Travel." JMIS, Fall 1991, pp. 53–79.

Copeland, D., and McKenney, J. "Airline Reservations Systems: Lessons from History." MIS Quarterly, Sept. 1988, pp. 353–370.

Duliba, K., Kauffman, R., and Lucas, H. C., Jr. "Airline CRS, Agency Automation Strategies and the 'Halo' Effect." Center for Research on Information Systems Working Paper no. IS-94–3, Stern School, New York University, 1994.

Chapter Five

Virtual Markets: Making Electronic Connections with Stakeholders

In this chapter, the IT design variables of *virtual components, electronic linking, electronic customer/supplier relations,* and *electronic workflows* are illustrated in the efforts of five organizations to develop *electronic markets.*

Markets—places where buyers and sellers meet to exchange goods and services—are fundamental to our economy. Economists argue that free markets are the most efficient for both the buyer and seller. In this chapter, we see the dramatic impact information technology has when it is used to create electronic markets.

The Nature of Markets

What do economists mean when they talk about efficient markets? In the securities markets, efficiency means that all relevant information about a security, say a share of common stock in AT&T, is known to the buyers and sellers. Therefore, no one has an unfair advantage in buying or selling AT&T shares. The reverse situation would arise if, for example, a person knew that AT&T was about to be awarded a major contract and could predict that its stock would rise in price. If no one else had this information, he or she might purchase shares at a favorable price from an unsuspecting seller. In the United States, companies have to be very careful about such announcements that will affect stock prices, so that information is available equally to all parties in the market.

While electronic markets cannot stop violations of insider trading regulations, they do make it much easier for legitimate buyers and sellers to get the information they need about products and services and to get it in a timely manner. Thus, an electronic market can be more efficient than a traditional one.

As an example of the general workings of markets, the securities markets are probably the easiest to understand. There is a bid price and an ask price quoted by the specialist, or market-maker. This person is willing to buy a security at one price and sell it at another, slightly higher price. The difference between the two prices is the market-maker's spread.

Practitioners in the securities markets are divided on how efficient the traditional securities market actually is. Many firms provide extensive research on industries and companies so that buyers can be more informed about companies in which they might want to invest. You, as an individual investor, might be willing to pay for information about companies on the stock market or for up-to-the-minute data on stocks. When you look for information about a product or service you incur a search cost; this cost is one of the buyer's expenses in using a market. The seller also has expenses in making you aware of a product or service and in providing information about it.

Costs of Using a Market

We often forget about the costs associated with an efficient market (costs of exchanging information), because we are so used to that market's operation, but consider this example. Suppose that you have decided to buy a new car. You might begin by reading about the cars that interest you in *Consumer Reports*. A year's subscription to this magazine costs only $22, and many libraries have copies. So far, your search cost is fairly low.

Then you visit a dealer and look at different models. After a tiring day of listening to salespeople and taking test drives, you finally choose a car. Now you have to buy it. You noticed that *Consumer*

Reports can fax you a detailed financial statement on specific car models showing a comparison of the sticker price with the dealer's invoice price, along with the sticker and dealer prices of various options. The cost of this service is $11. Since you dislike negotiating with the dealer, you order a price list for your chosen model.

Next it is time to go back to the dealer and get a firm price quotation. You visit one dealer and ask for his best price. You visit a second dealer and ask for her best price. You then mention that you have an offer that is a bit lower from another dealer and ask if she will beat it. Finally, you accept a price offer from this second dealer that is $100 less than that of the first dealer.

What are your costs of participating in this market now?

A subscription to *Consumer Reports* at $22.

The purchase of a report on the dealer's costs at $11.

One-half person-day of time doing initial research.

One person-day of time doing research while visiting dealers.

One person-day of time negotiating with dealers.

The costs will vary depending on how much you value your time; still, in monetary terms, your market costs were not too high.

What costs did the dealer incur on the seller's side of the market?

A sales building.

A salesforce.

Clerical and administrative personnel.

A computer system.

Advertising.

The dealer incurs substantial costs to participate as a seller in the new-car market.

Closed Market Hierarchies

Early economists tended to ignore the costs of markets and look just at the price a consumer was willing to pay for goods and services and the price at which a firm was willing to sell them. Then an economist named Oliver Williamson (1975) argued that there were costs from operating the market, which he called *transactions costs*. Williamson suggested that one way firms avoided transactions costs was by developing a market hierarchy. Instead of entering a market to buy a product, a firm might decide to make the product in-house, in effect creating a market in which it was the sole producer and consumer. Or the firm might even buy the supplier of the product. In either case, the firm would take on a more hierarchical structure. *Market hierarchies*, then, refer to closed markets with few participants, possibly one or two suppliers.

General Motors is an excellent example of a company that favors hierarchical markets, making some 70 percent of the parts in its cars. It bought Fisher Body company rather than negotiate with a supplier to build bodies for its cars, and its acquisition of goods and services through a market hierarchy has led to its vertical integration within its industry. However, within the same industry, Chrysler has chosen the opposite path and makes only about 30 percent of the parts in its cars.

What conditions are likely to lead to using a market hierarchy rather than a more public market? If an asset is highly specific to the firm, it is likely that no market exists for it. In other words, if you need a specialized piece of equipment or highly specialized skills, there may be no place to buy it. ABZ, the electronic components manufacturer mentioned earlier, which fabricates its products out of ceramic materials, has built most of the machines on its production line. There are only a few competitors in the world for ABZ's product, and there is no one who supplies production equipment specially tailored to its manufacturing needs. The firm had little choice but to hire engineers and invent its own manufacturing equipment. If there are few firms that can supply the goods or services you need, it is advantageous to work closely with the suppliers rather than look for the lowest bidder.

Another condition leading to the use of a hierarchy in place of a more open market is the need to purchase a complex product. A share of GM stock is easy to describe and one share is just as good as another. But if a buyer is looking for a large computer network that features local area and wide area connections, he or she will confront a variety of complex products and product descriptions. Malone, Yates, and Benjamin (1987) suggest that when one has a highly specific asset and/or a complex product description, goods are most likely to be purchased through a hierarchy. If the product is simple and nonspecific, buyers and sellers are most likely to be meeting in the marketplace.

Enter the Electronic Market

When a firm decides to develop and use its own hierarchy for acquiring goods and services, its transactions costs may be lowered, but it builds in overhead, an overhead that is likely to continue even if business shrinks. The firm must either continue to pay employees who have little to do or lay them off; both actions involve far more costs than simply reducing one's purchases from a supplier. With the emphasis today on just-in-time manufacturing, reducing overhead, and operational efficiencies, there is a tendency away from hierarchies and toward electronic markets, so that when a firm finds its sales dropping, it can reduce its orders to its suppliers.

Another disadvantage for firms with market hierarchies is that they can begin to loose the competitive benefits of the marketplace. When goods come from inside your firm, you may not test prices from other suppliers, and it is easy to become your own high-price producer. Again, General Motors offers a good example of this phenomenon; it has a very high cost structure arising from its history of vertical integration and internal manufacturing of parts. The recent popularity of outsourcing computer operations shows the opposite phenomenon. Firms doing this outsourcing have decided that their internal cost structures are too high compared to what the market has to offer.

Thus, it is likely that business will be moving toward making more acquisitions from the market and away from hierarchies. Information technology can accelerate this trend by helping to make markets more efficient (through the sharing of information) and by lowering transactions costs.

IT contributes to the marketplace and makes markets more efficient in a number of different ways. The possibilities range across a continuum from minor improvements in markets all the way to fully electronic markets.

What can IT contribute short of a totally electronic market? First, technology can help reduce search costs by making massive amounts of information available on-line. When you can access an on-line database of information about the products you want to purchase, it becomes easier to acquire needed information. National networks like Prodigy, CompuServe, and America Online provide some of this information in the United States. The Minitel network in France is a much better example as it contains data on many different types of products one can purchase. AT&T is starting a service in which customers will be able to program software agents to roam through a network; you could send an agent out to find a specific product or service from a number of vendors and to report back on its search.

The technology of electronic linking is a second way to make markets more efficient. Electronic data interchange (EDI) is extremely popular for reducing transactions costs while increasing accuracy and quality in purchasing goods. In a non-EDI environment, a customer typically places an order through its purchasing system by having data keyed into a computer. The system then generates a printed order that goes to the supplier of the product being ordered; the supplier has the printed order keyed into its order entry system. The keying and rekeying of data continues through change orders, shipping notices, and the payment cycle. The objective of EDI is to reduce this manual keying, reduce errors, and speed up the order and production cycle by allowing firms to exchange data electronically rather than in printed form.

Currently, EDI networks have had less impact than one would expect because firms often do not share standard, or compatible, telecommunications protocols. As a result, using EDI effectively across companies takes more expertise and resources than would be needed if everyone adhered to a communications standard. It is estimated that fewer than 1 percent of U.S. firms now use EDI applications.

Also, if a firm is involved in a nonstandard EDI network, then it is being pulled in two directions at once. Its EDI system means it is less dependent on a market hierarchy for purchasing, but the lack of a standard makes it hard to switch suppliers. It might have to redesign its EDI application before it can bring in new suppliers. However, if an industry, or even a country, were to adopt a standard, perhaps like the ANSI X.12 EDI protocol, then bringing new suppliers into the marketplace would become much easier. Just as standards have made the world's telephone systems interoperative, EDI standards have great promise for creating electronic marketplaces in which firms can easily offer and purchases goods and services (EDI and networks are discussed further in Chapter Eleven).

Baxter Healthcare's Electronic Market

Baxter Healthcare is often cited as an example of a firm that has gained a competitive advantage through the use of information technology. Short and Venkatraman (1992) have reported on the long history of the IT efforts of first American Hospital Supply (AHS) and then Baxter. In 1963, over thirty years ago, AHS initiated a strategy of making it easier for customers to place orders. The initial effort featured prepunched cards and a card reader connected to a telephone line. The customer used the card reader to send an order on a deck of cards to AHS. At AHS, the machine receiving the telephone call punched a duplicate deck of cards, which were then processed through a computer-based order entry system.

This system, known as ASAP, grew over the years. By 1973, customers had terminals connected to an AHS computer through which they could place orders with the hospital supply firm on-line. By 1988, Baxter had purchased AHS, and its customers were demanding all-vendor systems. Buyers did not like having to deal with the various kinds of computer equipment and software of competing vendors, and it was costly to train personnel on a number of different ordering programs. Baxter responded with a product called Baxter Express, through which it proposed to accept orders for a variety of vendors. Baxter would route orders for its products to its own computer and orders for other vendors to a value-added service bureau mailbox. Other vendors would call in and retrieve their orders from this mailbox.

This all-vendor system received a somewhat lukewarm response from Baxter's competitors however. Many did not like the idea of trusting Baxter to represent their products in its order entry system. Now Baxter is joining with an industry consortium to create an open network for hospital supplies. The desires of customers and the change required in Baxter's strategy are precursors of future developments. Baxter had managed to gain an advantage by tying customers to its order entry system; the company made it very easy to place an order with Baxter and reduced the incentive for placing an order with a competitor. Its strategy for gaining a competitive advantage had worked well; but then it had to give up some of that advantage in order to satisfy customers. Now Baxter will compete on service rather than proprietary technology, and it has adopted a new strategy that is also dependent on IT.

Today, Baxter is using its technology to promote the concept of the "stockless hospital." Baxter guarantees delivery to any location in a hospital needing supplies; there is no need for a large central inventory, nor is there even much need for departmental inventories. Like Domino's Pizza, Baxter delivers. Its new program is an example of employing communications and computer technology for order entry and combining that process with a superb logistics system to create a virtual inventory for hospitals. The hospital no longer owns or manages an inventory, but it receives service that is just as responsive as an on-site physical inventory.

Baxter built marketing programs around its capabilities and offered consulting help and even materials management software to hospitals. It was a significant decision for the firm to offer a more open environment for purchasing with Baxter Express. And it is unlikely that Baxter's customers are unique; customers in other marketplaces are going to demand equal access and ubiquitous networks. The quality of the market is enhanced for all customers if they can reach all possible suppliers.

Proprietary, and therefore restrictive, systems for connecting firms provide an advantage to one partner but not the other. In most cases, the advantage will accrue to the supplier who can lock in a customer. In the future, there will be increasing pressures for standards and uniformity so that we can have truly efficient technology-enabled markets.

Electronic Securities Markets

The endpoint on the market continuum is the completely electronic market. In this market, buyers and sellers exchange pricing information and execute a transaction electronically. The best-known electronic markets are in the financial industry, where asset specificity is quite low, as described earlier.

NASDAQ, in the United States, and the London Stock Exchange both feature electronic markets. In the NASDAQ system (and also the London system), there are competing dealers, individuals who agree to post bid and ask prices for securities and honor a certain number of shares traded at those prices. Of course, the dealer must constantly watch movements in the market and adjust his or her bid/ask prices. To use this electronic market, a potential customer calls a brokerage firm that is a member of NASDAQ. The brokerage firm can tell the customer exactly what the bid and ask prices are at that moment and can submit a buy or sell order on behalf of the customer. This transaction occurs electronically in milliseconds. Because the entire marketplace is electronic, per-transaction costs are very low. Recently, however, there has been criticism of the size of the bid/ask spreads on NASDAQ, with a suggestion that dealers have agreed to keep the spread higher than other exchanges. It remains to be seen whether and how this dispute will be resolved. Also, the electronic network itself was expensive to develop and is costly to operate. However, if you compare it to the infrastructure needed for a physical stock exchange, the cost seems more reasonable.

Electronic markets can have a profound effect on the structure of organizations. In the case of EDI and just-in-time production, raw materials and work-in-process inventories shrink to the point that they become virtual components of the manufacturing process. A just-in-time plant does have some inventory, possibly a day's worth, but this amount is very small compared to inventories held in traditional approaches to production.

In 1987, the London Stock Exchange moved to an electronic market (a process called the "Big Bang"). As insurance, it spent heavily to remodel the exchange floor, too, but the electronic market proved so popular and convenient to use that firms quickly abandoned the physical exchange floor. In this case, we see a clear example of a physical reality becoming virtual (Clemons and Weber, 1990).

Electronic Cotton Market

Electronic markets exist in other places than the securities industry. As early as 1976, cotton producers in the American Southwest who were members of the Plains Cotton Cooperative Association developed TELCOT, an electronic market for trading cotton (this example is based in part on Lindsey, Cheney, Kasper, and Ives, 1990).

One of the major issues in an electronic market is determining product quality. In the case of a stock, quality is not important in the sense that one share of a company has the same quality as another similar share of the same company. In the case of cotton, the quality is determined by the U.S. Department of Agriculture. The resulting grade is entered into TELCOT so that the buyer can assess product quality before making a bid.

TELCOT has been in business for over fifteen years, and cooperative sales have grown from $50 million to $500 million a year. The system processes over 100,000 transactions on a typical day and has hit a peak of nearly a quarter of a million transactions in one day. The operating budget for TELCOT is over $5 million annually. This electronic market has had an interesting impact on the cooperative: it used to buy about 90 percent of its producers' crops itself. Now it acts more like a broker, buying only about 30 percent itself.

The system provides a great deal of information about the cotton market. A producer can display information on the quality and market value for its lots of cotton at any time. Buyers and producers can see what lots have sold recently, their quality, and the price per pound paid by the buyers. Buyers can access a large portion of the world's available cotton on the system.

The system has also greatly speeded up the market. Since transactions are executed quickly, a major order does not affect prices as much as it did before the system took effect. Lindsey, Cheney, Kasper, and Ives (1990) report that in 1989, buyers purchased over 385,000 bales of cotton in minutes at the prevailing asking price, a day on which over $100 million of cotton was traded. Most of the purchase was used to fill an order for the People's Republic of China. Before the system, this order could have taken weeks to fill.

Electronic Flower Auctions

The United States is by no means the leader in electronic markets. I have mentioned the London Stock Exchange, but one of the most interesting applications of information technology to markets is taking place in the Netherlands. The Westland region of Holland covers the triangle bounded by the Hague, Rotterdam, and the North Sea; this area produces the majority of Dutch flowers. Because the weather tends not to cooperate, most of the flowers are grown in greenhouses. There are over 4,600 growers in the Westland area.

The nineteenth century in Holland saw the invention of the Dutch auction, a method that clearly favors the seller of a product. In a Dutch auction, the price starts off at a high number and drops quickly until a buyer accepts the price. Flowers in Holland are sold this way through a number of auction houses, including Flower Auction Westland. Today, the auction is highly automated. Lots, consisting of fresh flowers or potted plants, move through a room, and each one stops below the auction clock. The clock starts off pointing at a high price; each tick moves the hand rapidly down to a lower price. The buyers sit in a gallery; when one pushes a button, the clock stops, and he or she has purchased that lot of flowers at the price pointed to by the clock hand (this example is based on Copeland, 1991).

In the early 1990s, Flower Auction Westland tested a project to videotape the lots of flowers and show them in a window on the face of the auction clock. The idea was to reduce the amount of handling involved in moving lots of flowers through the auction hall and to increase the capacity of the auction hall by increasing speed. The staff also felt that greater speed put more pressure on buyers, who then tended to buy at higher prices. Here technology has been used to create an electronic workflow.

The flowers are graded by inspectors when they arrive at the auction, so that a buyer is always able to see at least one quality rating when making a purchase. Many buyers also inspect the flowers prior to the start of the auction, and they rely on grower reputations as well.

The experimental video system has interesting implications for the marketplace. If you no longer have to see the physical flowers or plants, then why come to the auction at all? Why do you need a building except to receive and breakdown the flowers and then reassemble them by buyer? Can the physical auction be replaced with a virtual one, an electronic market for flowers? We do not know yet if this electronic market will develop further, but the technology exists to greatly extend the reach of the auction. Someday, buyers from all over the world may be able to participate in an electronic Flower Auction Westland.

Implications

What do organizations need to move toward more electronic markets? Primarily, they need networks. All the companies described in this chapter rely on networks to connect various computing devices together. Markets like the flower auction require high bandwidth networks, that is, networks that have a very high transmission capability and can carry high-quality video and graphics in addition to text (networking is discussed further in Chapter Eleven).

In this chapter, we have seen how information technology is reinforcing a movement away from closed market hierarchies and toward open markets (Table 5.1 summarizes the key IT design variables used by each firm). Pressure for this movement comes from an urge to reduce overhead and to remain flexible as market conditions fluctuate. IT enables the creation of more efficient markets, that is, markets in which all the information needed is known to both buyer and seller.

Electronic markets and the linkages they allow between organizations also contribute greatly to the efficiency of the T-Form organization. The T-Form structure will make extensive use of *electronic linking and communications* to create interorganizational

Table 5.1. IT Design Variables and Markets.

IT Design Variable	Example
Electronic linking and communications	Baxter Healthcare; TELCOT; NASDAQ; London Stock Exchange
Electronic customer/supplier relationships	NASDAQ; London Stock Exchange; TELCOT—links between themselves and customers
Electronic workflows	Flower Auction Westland, as lots move through the auction
Virtual components	Baxter Healthcare, the stockless hospital

systems. An electronic marketplace facilitates these linkages by acting as an intermediary between buyers and sellers; it assists firms in forming *electronic customer/supplier relationships* and *virtual components*. As firms and industries adopt EDI standards, it will become easier to "plug in" to a central market and communicate electronically with other firms. Electronic markets will make up a central part of the external technology infrastructure that enables the T-Form organization.

Recommended Readings

Clemons, E., and Weber, B. "London's Big Bang: A Case Study of Information Technology, Competitive Impact and Organizational Change." *JMIS*, Spring 1990, pp. 41–60.

Copeland, D. "Flower Auction Westland: The COSMOS Project." Case study. London, Ont.: University of Western Ontario, 1991.

Lindsey, D., Cheney, P., Kasper, G., and Ives, B. "TELCOT: An Application of Information Technology for Competitive Advantage in the Cotton Industry." *MIS Quarterly*, Dec. 1990. pp. 347–357.

Short, J., and Venkatraman, N. "Beyond Business Process Redesign: Redefining Baxter's Business Network." *Sloan Management Review*, Fall 1992, pp. 7–21.

Chapter Six

Radical Change: Redesigning the Organization

One of the most popular management topics today is business process redesign, or reengineering. This chapter discusses process redesign and its relation to organization design. Many of the IT design variables presented in Chapter Two are involved in putting business process redesign into operation. In particular, we will look at *technological leveling*, *electronic workflows*, *production automation*, *virtual components*, and *technological matrixing*. This chapter also argues that creating the T-Form organization is tantamount to re-engineering the entire organization.

What Is Reengineering?

Unfortunately, definitions of reengineering sometimes are circular. The experts in this field define reengineering as a redesign of some process that creates at least an order of magnitude improvement or cost savings over the existing process. An approach like this means that every reengineering process is a success by definition!

Hammer and Champy's definition (1993) is useful because it is not tied completely to an outcome: "Reengineering is the fundamental rethinking and radical redesign of business processes to achieve dramatic improvements in critical, contemporary measures of performance, such as cost, quality, service, and speed" (p. 32). This framework has four key words:

Fundamental: ask why the firm does things a certain way.

Radical: get to the root of a process; look for reinvention as opposed to making superficial changes or minor enhancements to what is already in place.

Dramatic: focus on achieving quantum leaps in performance. Reengineering is not about aiming for marginal or incremental improvements. Results like 10 percent improvements are not reengineering successes.

Processes: look at a business process. Traditional design often is centered on tasks, jobs, people, and structures. Reengineering centers on a business process, that is, a collection of activities that takes one or more kinds of inputs and produces some output of value.

In an earlier article, Hammer (1990) described the spirit of reengineering as "obliterating" rather than automating. He argues that systems developers have too often simply automated existing processes without thinking about the need for radical change, even the need to obliterate. Reengineering and incremental improvements to business processes can be thought of as endpoints on a continuum. In Figure 6.1, reengineering and radical change are on the right-hand side of the continuum; small enhancements to a process fall to the left. (Possibly obliteration is off the scale on the right!)

It is very likely that the middle of the continuum represents an area of maximum work for minimum payoff. Therefore, one contribution of reengineering is to call management's attention to the fact that designers should concentrate on either incremental improvements or the radical redesign of processes; working in the middle ground often results in high expenditures to automate an existing, inefficient process.

If reengineering creates such dramatic gains, why would an organization ever be satisfied with incremental improvements? Working on the reengineering side of the continuum is risky. Changes of great magnitude may even appear to some as doing violence to the organization. When management selects reengineer-

Figure 6.1. Continuum from
Incremental Improvements to Reengineering.

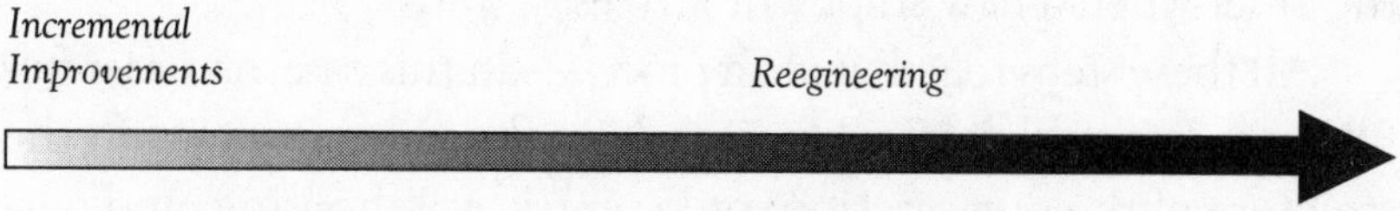

Incremental
Improvements   *Reengineering*

Accept current process.	Ask if process is necessary.
Look for ways to tune processes.	Look for radically different models.
Try to modify components of system.	Try to make changes that are dramatic: for example, cut labor 50%.
Avoid radical change and disruption.	Seek radical change in hopes of making significant improvements.

ing over incremental improvement, it is taking greater risks in the hope of obtaining greater benefits. The presence of these risks may explain why the history of the evolution of applications systems does not appear as a continual reengineering effort but is characterized by ongoing incremental improvements punctuated by major reengineering efforts.

Reengineering and IT Design Variables

Most of the chapters up to this point have focused on organization structure and how IT design variables can be used to change structures. The main contribution of reengineering to this discussion is to focus our attention on *processes* as opposed to structures.

What exactly is a process? One fundamental process for a firm that sells a product is order fulfillment. Picture a mail-order firm in which operators take orders when customers call a toll-free number. The order entry department is responsible for talking to customers and entering their orders into a computer system. The system checks a "book" inventory to determine if the goods requested are available. If so, it produces a picking list for the warehouse staff to use in completing the order. If the requested merchandise is out of stock, the system notifies the purchasing department that it is time to reorder, and it creates a backorder on the system so that the system can fill the order when a new shipment arrives.

All these steps together are a process—in this case, an order fulfillment process that cuts across at least three departments in the structure of the organization: order entry, warehousing, and purchasing. One objective for the T-Form organization is to be highly efficient; we want to see that the basic processes of the business are carried out efficiently regardless of how the firm may be structured.

Business process redesign is likely to employ four or five IT design variables. The radical reorganization of a process is likely to result in *technological leveling* as technology is used to reduce the need for multiple layers of management to be part of a process. Redesign, or reengineering, is also often associated with *production automation* and *electronic workflows* as well as *virtual components*. It may also introduce *technological matrixing*.

Reengineering a Process at Mutual Benefit Life

One of the early examples of reengineering was at Mutual Benefit Life Insurance Company (Hammer, 1990). Before its business process redesign, Mutual Benefit Life (MBL) processed life insurance applications in a long multistep process that included credit checking, quoting, rating, underwriting, and so on. An application might go through thirty steps across five departments; up to nineteen people could be involved. Typical turnarounds ranged from five to twenty-five days. Another firm estimated that a life insurance application spent twenty-two days in process for seventeen minutes of actual work (Hammer, 1990, p. 106).

To redesign this process, MBL used computer networks, databases, and an expert system to make information and decision support available to employees. It created the new position of case manager, a person who is a *process owner*. A case manager has total responsibility for an application from the time it is received until a policy is issued. Files are no longer handed from one person in the chain to another across departmental boundaries. Case managers are able to perform all of the tasks required to process an insurance application because they have technology to help them. An expert system provides advice while the case managers' PC-based work-stations connect to a variety of databases and applications on a mainframe computer.

What were the results? MBL can now complete an application in as little as four hours and the average time to turn around an application and issue a policy is two to five days. The company was able to eliminate 100 field office positions, yet its case managers can handle nearly twice the volume of applications that MBL could pre-viously process.

This example shows the use of production automation, in which workstations provide the information needed for an indi-vidual to make a decision. The workstation, mainframe computers, and network create a virtual applications processing workflow for each case worker. He or she has access to credit checks, quotations, ratings, and underwriting electronically rather than physically.

It is a sad footnote that MBL's investment performance was not as good as its reengineering; the company was taken over by the state of New Jersey. One has to be able to manage all aspects of the business to be successful!

Reengineering a Process at Merrill Lynch

My colleagues Don Berndt and Greg Truman and I (Lucas, Berndt and Truman, in press) have studied a reengineering project in the securities processing operation of Merrill Lynch, the largest bro-kerage and financial services firm in the United States, with over 500 branch offices. The objective of the securities processing oper-ation is to receive stock certificates from customers, perform the proper processing of the certificates, and post the resulting data to customer accounts.

The process flow is illustrated in high-level outline in Figure 6.2. On a typical day, Merrill Lynch branch offices around the United States receive some 3,500 securities, mailed or brought in by customers and requiring processing of some kind. Customers may bring securities to a branch office because the customer has sold the stock and must surrender it so that shares can be issued to the buyer; the customer has inherited stock and must have the shares registered in his or her name; a company has reorganized and has called in its old stock to issue new shares; a bond has been called in by the issuer; or the customer wants Merrill Lynch to hold his or her securities.

In the old process, after the customers brought their certificates to a branch office or sent them to Merrill Lynch through the mail, the branch conducted a manual review for negotiability. If this preliminary review verified that a security was negotiable, a clerk typed a receipt for the customer. If the certificates appeared not to be negotiable, the clerk told the customer what additional information was necessary to complete the transaction.

During the day, several branch clerks accepted certificates and accumulated them. At the end of the day, a courier took a package of all the certificates to one of two securities processing centers (SPCs) in Philadelphia or Chicago. The clerks attached a manually prepared manifest to the package summarizing its contents.

Normally, the package arrived at the SPC the next day. Upon its arrival, an SPC clerk inspected it and checked that its contents balanced with the manifest. The clerk contacted the branch office to resolve any discrepancies. All certificates that matched the manifest continued to the next stage in processing, which was to microfilm all certificates.

Next, clerks conducted a second negotiability review, which was contingent on the type of transaction: legal or nonlegal. An example of a legal transaction is the stock transfer that occurs when someone inherits a security. Regulations require that certain documents accompany the security certificate—for example, a death cer-

**Figure 6.2. Merrill Lynch
Securities Processing: Original System.**

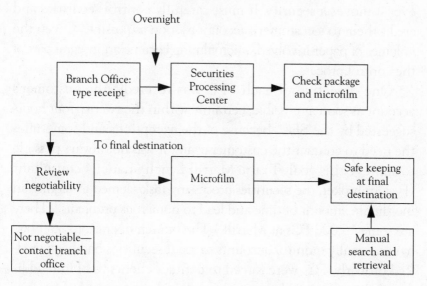

tificate for the person in whose name the security is currently registered. A nonlegal transaction, on the other hand, does not require legal documentation.

If further review showed the security certificate was not negotiable, it was segregated. If it was classified as negotiable, the certificate moved to a final holding area for distribution. A clerk logged the negotiability status into a Merrill Lynch securities control system.

The SPCs sent 80 to 90 percent of the certificates directly to depositories. The remaining certificates were distributed to specialty departments in New York for further processing: for example, one department handled exchanges of stock necessitated by a stock split. Upon arrival at a depository or at a Merrill specialty department, the certificates were again microfilmed and staff members updated their status in the control computer system. Certificates were microfilmed yet again before consignment to their final holding area.

The process entailed so much microfilming because Merrill

Lynch, like other brokers, is required by the Securities and Exchange Commission (SEC) to keep an accurate audit trail whenever it moves a security. It must carefully control securities and credit them to a customer's account as soon as possible. Given the volumes of paper involved, microfilming became an integral part of the control process.

One objective of each SPC was to credit the customer's account as soon as possible, certainly within the twenty-four hours suggested by the SEC. Because of the exceptions and sometimes the need to contact the customer again, it was not always possible to achieve this goal. To the Merrill Lynch financial consultant (FC), or broker, the securities processing task seemed to require an inordinate amount of time and lead to numerous problems. (There are some 15,000 FCs at Merrill.) The branch operations staff had to continually monitor accounts to see if securities had been credited properly. FCs were forced to contact clients to obtain additional documents. The process produced a great deal of friction between the sales side of the business and the securities processing department.

All these reasons plus the labor intensive nature of processing led to a desire to improve securities processing. The most radical approach would be to "obliterate" the process entirely, but this option was out of the control of Merrill Lynch. While there has been much publicity about "book entry" shares of stocks (an electronic record of ownership), there still are a large number of physical shares of stocks and bonds in circulation. Obliterating securities processing activity would require industry-level and government cooperation to eliminate all physical certificates, replacing them all with an electronic record. This solution would also require consumer acceptance and a massive effort to record electronically and then eliminate all existing paper certificates.

Since obliterating the process was not feasible, the systems group at Merrill Lynch, after hearing suggestions from the operations staff and doing extensive research, proposed a completely redesigned process using image technology to store an image of the security and the related documents that accompany it. The focus of the project was on workflow redesign, and it involved the closing of the two existing processing centers and the development of a securities processing department at a single site (originally in New York, now in New Jersey). The new process is outlined in Figure 6.3.

As in the old process, customers bring or mail securities to a branch office. The branch cashier conducts a preliminary negotiability review, but now he or she is supported by an expert system. This system not only helps the cashier determine negotiability status but also prints a customer receipt and generates a document control ticket that travels with the certificates. The expert system posts a record of the certificate to a computer file, including a unique identifier number for the transaction.

Figure 6.3. Merrill Lynch Securities Processing: New System.

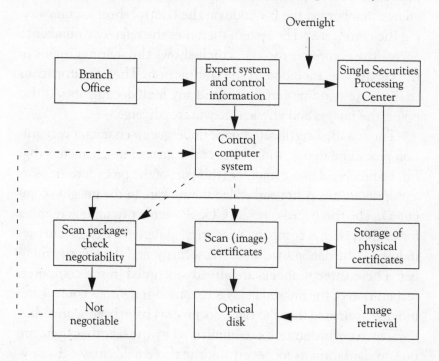

At the end of the day, clerks package all certificates to be taken by courier to the single SPC. The expert system generates a manifest sheet for the package and updates a manifest file so that it contains information on the shipment.

At the SPC, the staff first uses a wand to read a bar code on the package to verify receipt. Clerks check the package against the manifest; if there is a discrepancy they update the computer files, and the computer notifies the branch. Branch personnel have access to these files so that they can check the processing status of any security at any time. Negotiability must, of course, be verified in the new process. However, the presence of the expert system in the branches has reduced the number of certificates arriving without the documents needed for negotiability by 50 percent for legal transfers and 75 percent for nonlegals.

A major technological innovation in the process was the introduction of image scanning and character recognition for certain key fields on the stock certificate. The scanning system recognizes a reference number via the bar code on the control sheet accompanying the certificates. The system then uses the reference number to access the computer record, which shows the scanner operator the certificates included in the transaction. The operator scans in the corresponding certificates and any legal documents. At this point, the images and physical certificates diverge.

The scanned certificate image undergoes a character recognition procedure to turn three areas of the image into characters that can be processed by a computer (this part of the procedure employs a proprietary algorithm embedded in firmware in the imaging computer). The three areas are the CUSIP number (a unique number for each type of a company's security, assigned by the securities industry), the denomination of the security, and the security number. These three numbers are already recorded in the computer; recognition of the imaged fields is to establish rigorous control and provide assurance that the right documents have been scanned.

The recognition task is complicated by the fact that there are no standard formats for securities; the three fields may exist anyplace on the security, but the recognition algorithm needs to know where to look for the fields it is trying to convert. That information comes from a template database that indicates where the three fields are located on each particular kind of security. Merrill has developed a template for each CUSIP and date of issue combination. The scanning computer routes any certificate whose template is not yet in the database to a workstation operator. The operator uses a mouse to draw a box around each field, and the system records this location information in a new template for the security.

The system performs the image-to-character conversion by referencing the stored image, overlaying the template, and executing the algorithm. If the converted character fields match the fields already in the computer, the system updates the computer files to show that scanning has been completed and stores the images for this transaction permanently to optical disk. If there is a mismatch between the converted characters and the computer record, or other nonrecognition, the system refers the transaction to the key edit area. There, operators examine the image and input data to unrecognized fields.

Staff then take the physical certificates for distribution to their final location. The system executes a procedure to provide routing orders for each certificate and also specifies a destination box for the certificate.

When a user needs access to security information, he or she can retrieve the image of the security on a graphics workstation. There is no need to access the physical security or to hunt through microfilm records, a process that could take as long as three days in the old process.

Table 6.1 outlines the major changes in the Merrill Lynch SPC process, including the elimination of the two old process centers and the creation of a securities processing department at a central site. The new process supports major changes in tasks and workflow, beginning with the receipt of securities at a branch office. The interface to the process for all groups having contact with it has also been changed.

Table 6.1. Outline of Merrill Lynch Process Changes.

Preparation Action	Motivation
Organization structure	Elimination of two securities processing centers and consolidation of all securities processing in a central site
Workflows and functions	New branch office input New branch office customer receipt Anticipated receipt information New package receipt and bar coding Elimination of most microfilming Revised legal negotiability workflow Use of imaging operation (scanning and key edit) Retrieval of image rather than physical security
Interface	Branch office interface Customer interface Worker interface with scanning equipment User interface in retrieving images

Technology	Expert system added to assist branch cashier receiving certificates
	Scanning incorporated to replace most microfilm and provide better control, requiring:
	    Scanners
	    Template definition
	    Key edit
	    Computer facility with optical disk jukebox
	    Retrieval of scanned documents
	    Modifications to existing control system

Impact	Improvements in customer service:
	    Better customer receipt
	    More information captured at point of contact
	    Broker ability to query status of processing
	    Better control
	Improvements in certificate-level control:
	    High-quality images compared to spotty microfilm
	    Up to three-day searches reduced to instantaneous retrieval
	    Significant cost reduction
	    Reduction in research time

Source: Lucas, Berndt, and Truman, in press.

Technology changes include the expert system for the branch office input, scanners, a template library, character recognition from images, and optical disk storage. There have been significant increases in the level of customer service and the quality of support securities processing provides to the branches. There is much less handling of physical securities and retrieval time for a certificate image is nearly instantaneous. The time to research a security has been dramatically reduced; from up to three days in the old process to virtually instantaneously in the new.

The new securities processing system has had a dramatic impact on resources: reduction of occupancy from two locations to one, reduction in depository fees, interest savings on receivables, reduction of microfilm costs, savings on security services, reduction in staff of 168 positions leaving a current total of 165 including temporary staff.

The new process required an investment of approximately $3 million. The return on the investment was calculated as a payback period of less than two years, which translates to a savings of around $1.5 million a year.

This example shows how management can execute a major redesign of a business process. Merrill Lynch used technology along with process redesign for technological leveling, reducing the number of processing centers and the number of managers and workers needed to staff them. It applied information technology to automating the flow of certificates through the SPC, a form of production automation. It developed electronic workflows, for example, the image system captures the certificates electronically, employees in different departments can retrieve the image of a certificate in seconds without the need to visit a vault, and the certificate image can be routed to any Merrill Lynch terminal capable of displaying it. (As of this writing, Merrill Lynch is in the process of outsourcing all securities handling to a third party; the simplification of securities processing has made it possible for Merrill Lynch to turn over all handling of securities to a separate firm that will use electronic linking and communications to work as a partner with Merrill Lynch.)

Reengineering the Entire Firm at Oticon

The Merrill Lynch redesign of security processing illustrates how management can use business process redesign to make substantial changes in one part of an organization. This next example illustrates how process redesign, or reengineering, can affect the fundamental structure of an organization.

Bjorn-Andersen and Turner (1994) and Gould and Stanford (1994) have written about the changes at the Danish company Oticon. The firm is one of the five largest hearing aid manufacturers in the world, with about 1,200 employees and sales of $80 million. Oticon has its own research department and production facilities and exports more than 90 percent of its production to over 100 countries. It has positioned itself to be the preferred partner for leading hearing aid clinics around the world.

Company headquarters is in the Tuborg industrial park to the North of Copenhagen. There are three manufacturing facilities, located in Denmark and other countries.

The company began producing hearing aids during World War II. It was family owned until 1956, when new management took over and began mass production of hearing aids. By the end of the 1970s, Oticon had reached the number one position in the world market, with a 15 percent market share and sales in over 100 countries. It was a leader in miniaturization for hearing aids worn behind the ear.

From 1979 through 1985, Oticon's market share dropped from 15 percent to 7 percent as competitors developed hearing aids that fit inside the ear. The company had losses in 1986 and 1987, leading the board to bring in new management.

A new president, Lars Kolind, came to Oticon in 1988. His first action was to start a cost-cutting program in an attempt to regain profitability. Kolind also changed the firm's marketing strategy. For years, Oticon had stressed high-quality hearing aids, but now competitors were also building quality units. Kolind decided that the most appropriate strategy for Oticon was quality *and* customer satisfaction. Oticon would focus its business on dispensers or retailers of hearing aids who were most interested in producing satisfied customers.

After two years, Kolind realized that cost cutting and a new marketing strategy had accomplished about all they could. "I sat down on New Year's Day . . . and tried to think the unthinkable; a vision for the company of tomorrow. It would be a company where jobs were shaped to fit the person instead of the other way around. Each person would be given more functions and a job would emerge by the individual accumulating a portfolio of functions" (Bjorn-Andersen and Turner, 1994).

Kolind wanted to transform Oticon from an industrial organization producing a standardized product to a "high quality service organization with a physical product." He envisioned an organization in which various functional units worked together in an integrated manner to develop innovative products, and he realized that he would have to create a new, flexible organization.

Kolind wrote a memo describing Oticon as one team of 150 employees at headquarters, all continuously developing and learning new skills. Each employee should be able to do several tasks; those he or she already did well and those where he or she would be challenged to learn new tasks. The idea was not to focus on functional expertise but to have each person be able to do several jobs. Kolind also felt that paper hindered efficiency, that paper hides information instead of sharing it. He imagined computer systems that would eliminate paper and allow all employees to share information.

Kolind called his new plan a "spaghetti organization" because he envisioned people playing multiple intertwined roles in the firm. To begin with, he combined two separate offices and placed them into a new building designed for his new organization. Unlike the leaders in many business process redesign projects, Kolind invited the participation of his employees in designing the new organization. But at first, there was a great deal of resistance to his proposals. However, when Kolind backed off a plan to move headquarters to Jutland, a remote part of Denmark, and chose instead to locate in the Tuborg industrial park, resistance faded. Overall, it is clear that the changes described below would not have happened without Kolind's strong and forceful leadership.

Having eliminated traditional departments in the head office, he then organized work as projects. Oticon views projects as temporary assignments; employees with different skills work together on different projects only for as long as they are needed. This team-oriented arrangement works very well when the workload is uneven. For example, in a rigid structure, the marketing department would be permanently staffed to handle its heavy load in the fall for exhibitions and trade shows. In a project-oriented structure, such seasonal marketing tasks become projects and enough resources are assigned to complete them. Normally, about five people work consistently on marketing tasks at Oticon; when the busy season arrives, this core group recruits other employees with different backgrounds, such as R&D, to help out.

For each project at headquarters, there is a project manager who has responsibility for staffing the team and for carrying out the task. The project manager advertises the project on an electronic bulletin board on the Oticon system; employees sign up for a project from their workstations. Each employee occupies several positions at Oticon, the number depends on the number and variety of projects for which he or she volunteers. This approach to organizing takes maximum advantage of diversity; an employee in accounting might sign up for a project involving marketing, bringing a whole new perspective to the marketing project.

To be successful at this reengineering effort that changes its organization structure, Oticon has had to adopt a new philosophy of control. Management has to trust employees to sign up for projects; this voluntarism should result in greater commitment to the firm and more worker responsibility. Managers spend less time monitoring workers; instead, managers must be innovators and motivators.

Oticon has also had to rearrange its physical and technology domains. First, Kolind eliminated all private offices, including his own. All employees have identical desks and chairs in a large open space. Each desk has a workstation and a mobile phone charger. Desks are not assigned. Workers bring small lockable caddies to whatever desk they are using. The caddie has a drawer for personal items and shelves for storing up to ten personal files. Access to information is gained through the workstation.

Kolind also wanted to banish paper; Oticon's technology has eliminated 95 percent of the paper in the office. The company scans all documents as they are received, and employees are prohibited from keeping paper files. Original documents are shredded. All of the information from these documents is stored in electronic form, and users can retrieve it from their workstations, given that they have access rights. When an employee enters his or her ID into the workstation, the system is configured with that individual's electronic desktop. The system has tools for creating, transmitting, and storing documents containing text, drawings, and graphics. This combination of physical and electronic flexibility makes it possible to create task forces almost immediately to solve a problem.

Oticon has enjoyed a return to profitability; 1992 profits were nine times better than those of 1989 and 1990. Sales are increasing, and the company has reduced its cycle time to market new products. A new hearing aid that adjusts itself to the level of ambient sound was brought to market six months earlier than it could have been in the old organization.

Oticon's reengineering demonstrates technological leveling in the reduction of layers of management and the substitution of IT-supported workgroups. Information technology helps form the project teams, facilitates communications, and provides tools to team members to accomplish their tasks. This approach also changes the role of the manager, making him or her much more a leader than a person who monitors employees. Since employees work on many different projects, the company also illustrates technological matrixing.

Oticon has created a highly flexible and virtual organization through process redesign combined with the use of several IT design variables. It is a good example of a firm that is making progress toward the T-Form organization. It also shows how reengineering can be applied at the level of the firm.

Reengineering the Entire Firm at Lithonia Lighting

This last example of reengineering also involves an entire organization, though perhaps others would not call what took place reengineering since it occurred before that term was in general use. Lithonia Lighting was founded in 1946 in Lithonia, Georgia (this example is described in Berkley, 1992). The current senior management team arrived in the early 1960s to a strong but regional company. There were few national firms in the industry, and Lithonia was no exception; it had sales of $18 million and was strongest in the Southeast.

Management embarked on a strategy of becoming the number one lighting supplier in the United States. Most of the necessary growth was internal, though management did buy a few other companies. By 1990, an industry of over 1,300 companies had coalesced into nine major manufacturers of lighting fixtures who accounted for 75 percent of industry sales. In 1990, Lithonia had sales of over $700 million.

The lighting industry has complex distribution channels. Lighting can consume 50 percent of the electricity in a commercial building, and architects work with contractors to manage this kind of energy consumption. Most of Lithonia's products are aimed at the commercial lighting industry, which means its customers are industrial builders, not end users. Architects, contractors, electrical engineers, distributors, and agents are involved in Lithonia's sales.

In 1979, the information systems (IS) manager at Lithonia was asked to find a way to tie together all of the major players in Lithonia's business, including agents, distributors, contractors, warehouses, and so on. The IS manager's team soon found that it had to take Lithonia out of the center of its diagrams; the only picture that made any sense put the *agent* at the center of the diagram.

This exercise convinced Lithonia to change the way it looked at its business: the agent became the key to sales. Lithonia deals with about eighty-five independent lighting agencies. An agent sells to distributors, who, in turn, sell fixtures off the shelf. However, the majority of agency sales come from efforts to influence the buyers for a large construction project, like a new office building. Specifically, it is the electrical contractor of a construction project who makes the ultimate decisions on what fixtures to buy. The agents do not stock products, nor do they carry inventory. Also, agents tend not to handle competing products.

Once it decided to focus its strategy on agents, Lithonia developed a series of innovative computer and communications applications called Light*Link to coordinate sales and distribution. The high level of cooperation between the CEO and IS manager at Lithonia in carrying out this development won an award from the Society for Information Management, SIM.

The general assessment of the Light*Link system is that it generated considerably increased sales volume without a concomitant increase in staff. In fact, one agency reduced its sales representative to administrative staff ratio from 1:1 to 3:1. And Lithonia has credited the system with dramatic gains in sales. (Of course, we should be cautious about such claims because sales are primarily determined by the health of the construction industry.)

Lithonia developed its new concept of business before anyone had invented reengineering or business process redesign. In retrospect, however, it seems to be a clear case of a firm's redesigning itself and its processes in keeping with a fresh view of the environment. The Light*Link system provided a number of electronic workflows and the ability to communicate easily with Lithonia. To some extent, the systems also provided production automation, as computers were able to generate some quotations and specifications for customers.

Implications

Mutual Benefit Life and Merrill Lynch represent classic cases of reengineering, of business process redesign (see Table 6.2). Reengineering's major contribution to management is its focus on process and on asking whether or not a particular process is necessary. Both MBL and Merrill Lynch began by looking at certain areas of their own businesses in detail. The specific questions that one should ask include:

- What are our key business processes?
- Do we have to execute this particular process at all?
- What totally new ways, taking advantage of information technology, exist to perform this process?
- What does redesigning this process imply for the structure of the organization?
- How can we use IT design variables in conjunction with process redesign to change the structure of the organization?

Oticon and Lithonia practiced a different kind of reengineering; they focused on the entire organization instead of isolated business processes. In their reengineering efforts, these firms used *technological leveling* to reduce the number of layers of management

Table 6.2. IT Design Variables and Reengineering.

IT Design Variable	Example
Electronic workflows	Mutual Benefit, claims routing; Merrill Lynch, securities routing and retrieval; Lithonia Lighting, bids and quotes
Production automation	Mutal Benefit, claims; Merrill Lynch, securities processing
Technological leveling	Merrill Lynch, reduction in SPC employment; Oticon, multiskilled staff at headquarters
Technological matrixing	Lithonia Lighting, relationship with agents; Oticon, task forces
Virtual components	Oticon, shifting departments and task forces

and supervision. They substituted *electronic workflows* for the physical movement of documents, and they applied *production automation* where possible. *Technological matrixing* helped solve problems and encouraged employees to make decisions themselves rather than refer problems up a managerial hierarchy. All these changes combined produced organizations with *virtual components*.

Since reengineering is very popular today, it may make some sense to view creating the T-Form organization as a reengineering exercise aimed at the entire organization rather than a single business process. Reengineering the organization using the IT design variables presented earlier falls at the radical end of our change continuum. It is because the T-Form organization does represent radical change, that firms that adopt this structure should gain a tremendous advantage over competitors who retain their traditional organization structures.

Recommended Readings

Berkley, J. "Lithonia Lighting." Case study. Boston: Harvard Business School, 1992.

Bjorn-Andersen, N., and Turner, J. "Creating the 21st Century Organization: The Metamorphosis of Oticon." Paper presented at the IFIP Working Group 8.2 Conference, Ann Arbor, Mich., Aug. 1994.

Davenport, T. *Process Innovation: Reengineering Work Through Information Technology*. Boston: Harvard Business School Press, 1993.

Gould, R. M., and Stanford, M. *Revolution at Oticon A/S (A&B)*. Lausanne, Switzerland: IMD, 1994.

Lucas, H. C., Jr., Berndt, D., and Truman, G. "Reengineering: A Framework for Evaluation and Case Study of an Imaging System." *Communications of the ACM*, in press.

Part Three

Designing the T-Form Organization

Part Three of *The T-Form Organization* illustrates the use of IT design variables in specific kinds of organization and process redesign. Each example shows how a company has used one or more IT design variables to make major changes in the way it does business. Chapter Seven is devoted to change at the level of the entire organization; the firms described in this chapter have used IT design variables as the basis for their structure or in a major restructuring effort. They have employed electronic communications and linking and have created virtual components. Some have used electronic workflows to reduce cycle times. In each company, the use of technology has substituted for layers of management, an example of technological leveling.

Chapter Eight looks at the operations process in detail. All companies have some activities that can be classified as operations, even a professional firm has an operations process to deliver its services. This chapter shows the use of IT design variables to improve operations, frequently through electronic communications and linking and partnerships to form virtual components. Technology is used heavily here to reduce cycle times and eliminate paper processing.

One popular strategy for competing is to provide outstanding customer service, the topic of Chapter Nine. Here, too, IT design variables play a part. The three companies described in this chapter make extensive use of electronic customer/supplier relationships to provide outstanding customer service. As firms try to become more efficient and reduce their cycle times, they depend on suppliers to provide high levels of service and reduced cycle times, too. A huge manufacturing plant that relies on just-in-time inventory can be shut down if a key supplier is a few hours late with a shipment. As a result, many supplier firms have found they can charge a premium price if they combine a product with high levels of service. IT design variables help create organizations structured to provide superior customer service.

Until the development of groupware, information technology had made rather modest contributions to the everyday activities of managers. Groupware is computer software is aimed at the fundamental tasks of management: communications, the sharing of information, coordinating individuals and groups, and seeing that the knowledge in the organization is applied where it is needed. Groupware clearly supports electronic linking and communications, and technological matrixing. Its information sharing and communications capabilities allow managers to form temporary workgroups and matrix structures. It should make possible larger spans of control and contribute to technological leveling. Chapter Ten discusses this emerging application of technology and its profound implications for the design of organizations.

Chapter Seven

Technology-Based Structures: New Organizational Forms

IT design variables can be used to create new and innovative organization structures. This chapter focuses on the IT design variables of *technological leveling, electronic linking and communications, electronic workflows*, and *virtual components* as they are used today in three companies. While there are few examples of companies that have relied solely on these design variables in structuring themselves, these three firms illustrate how you can use IT design variables to supplement or to substitute for traditional design variables.

Nontraditional Organization Design at Mrs. Fields Cookies

Mrs. Fields Cookies is an oft-cited example of a firm that has used information technology as a part of its organization structure (this example draws upon Ostrofsky, 1988, and the articles cited below). Mrs. Fields Cookies, begun in 1977, is a chain of small retail outlets, typically located in shopping malls. Until recently, the focus was on selling several varieties of cookies and a few other selected food items. In 1988, when the emphasis was still on cookies, there were approximately 500 retail stores worldwide. Stores follow a formula of consistent, uniform quality and price regardless of location.

Mrs. Fields Cookies has a unique structure: two parallel organizations, one of which has a traditional span of control while the other has a very broad span of control. Until recently, every shop was wholly owned by the company rather than franchised, and the company was under the strong centralized control of Debbie Fields and her husband, Randy Fields. The unique organization of Mrs. Fields Cookies allowed the owners maximum flexibility in adapting their offerings to the changing tastes of customers in a "fad" business.

In 1988, the traditional hierarchical organization was formed by 500 store managers, 105 district sales managers, seventeen regional directors, four senior regional directors, a vice president of operations, and finally, Debbie Fields. The average span of control in this hierarchy is about 1:5.

The second organization is a formal reporting relationship for control purposes; here, in 1988, 500 store managers reported to six store controllers, who reported to the vice president of operations. The span of control between controllers and store managers ranges from 1:35 to 1:75, which represents a very flat organization structure. Thus, the "human" side of management at Mrs. Fields is through a traditional hierarchy; the "numbers" side is a flat organization made possible through information technology.

Randy Fields was an IBM systems engineer at one point in his career. At Mrs. Fields, the opportunity to design a new organization combined with a senior manager with extensive experience with technology led to a design in which the IT variables we have been discussing were used to create a nontraditional structure.

IT is an integral part of the structure of Mrs. Fields Cookies. Each store is connected on-line to a central database, and there is extensive automation of production quotas, sales volumes, and so on, based on recent daily sales records for each store. Each store is given hourly sales projections and reports hourly sales results. All ordering of supplies (for example, chocolate chips and other baking needs) is done automatically from the central database with direct delivery to the store.

Each store's product mix, sales quotas, and special promotions are customized by an expert system that adapts to hourly sales. The company also uses IT for coordination; through voice mail and electronic mail, each store manager has direct personal interaction with

Debbie Fields herself. Companywide announcements are frequently broadcast to each store by voice mail, significantly personalizing these announcements compared to memos and reports. (Debbie Fields was a cheerleader in high school, and voice mail seemed a natural way to rally the troops.) Each manager may send Debbie Fields electronic messages for particular problems and expect a personal response within forty-eight hours.

Comments by employees about Randy Fields illustrate the philosophy of top management. Paul Quinn, director of management information systems, has said, "We are all driven by Randy's philosophy that he wants the organization to be as flat as possible." Controller Lynn Quilter has said, "There are a few things that Randy dislikes about growth. . . . He hates the thought of drowning in people so that he can't walk in and know exactly what each person does. . . . The second thing that drives him nuts is paper." Fields himself has remarked that "the objective is to leverage people—to get them to act when we have 1,000 stores the same way they acted when we had 30." He has also observed that, as a rule, "if a machine can do it, a machine *should* do it. People should do only that which people can do. It's demeaning for people to do what machines can do." However, another rule is to have only one database. Fields has said that if this second rule is not enforced, "the next thing you know you have 48 different programs that can't talk to each other" (Richman, 1987, p. 67).

Technological leveling has allowed Mrs. Fields to reduce boundaries between stores and headquarters; the technology has created an organization structure that feels flat despite having many layers of management. Electronic linking and communications make it easy to communicate across time zones using voice and e-mail. The technology also affects the nature of work because it supplies detailed store operational control, freeing personnel for more sales work. Mrs. Fields can be more responsive to customers; it can change products and product mix through the systems running at headquarters and in the stores.

There have, however, been management problems. The firm expanded rapidly, possibly encouraged by the success of its technology, and ran into difficulty integrating an acquisition, La Petite Boulangerie (a bakery and café). While Mrs. Fields can change its mix of cookies easily, the original cookie operation is basically a one-product business. The firm is also reported to have had difficulties with its product and market mix when it entered international markets.

In 1988, Mrs. Fields Cookies lost money for the first time, and its stock fell dramatically on the London Exchange. "The PCs that brought revolutionary management techniques to cookie stores weren't able to overcome the basic business realities of a limited, fickle market," suggested an article in *PC Week* (1989). The article went on to describe a risky strategy in which Mrs. Fields was "betting the company" that its cookie-store systems could save the organization. According to Randy Fields, Mrs. Fields entered the bakery business because it was confident that its computer systems would make it possible to get control of La Petite Boulangerie. The company planned to spend $50 million on the bakery chain in the early 1990s, closing 100 of its 700 cookie stores and converting them to combined bakeries and cookie stores. Randy Fields noted that the company was investing further in the bakery chain because it had been so successful in installing its computer systems that the bakeries had been profitable within fourteen months of the chain's purchase.

Unfortunately, Mrs. Fields Cookies had a net loss of $8.8 million in 1990. In 1991, trading of its stock was suspended pending restructuring of a $70 million debt. Undeterred by debt, in 1992, Mrs. Fields Cookies and Pasteleria el Molino announced a leasing agreement to open fifty stores in Mexico over a five-year period.

In May of 1992, Debbie Fields launched Mrs. Fields Ice Cream, to be sold in supermarkets, not cookie stores. She also started Mrs. Fields Mini Cookie Store, a cart equipped with a cookie-baking oven, designed to be set up in grocery stores. In 1992, Mrs. Fields had over 700 cookie stores; over 5,000 employees; stores in thirty-five states, Bangkok, Hong Kong, Japan, Australia, Canada, and Great Britain; ten locations on the Pennsylvania Turnpike, in carts; and plans to launch lower-fat cookies and cookie dough in ready-to-bake packages.

In November of 1992, Jesse Ewing, vice president of operations for Mrs. Fields, and his wife became one of the first Mrs. Fields franchisers. (Prior to this time, Debbie Fields had refused to franchise, wanting to own all of the stores.) Ewing paid an initial $25,000 franchise fee, and $200,000 for construction and equipment for a store.

Meanwhile, also in 1992, Randy Fields spun off a company called ROI, which specializes in selling the software made famous at Mrs. Fields. He stepped down as chairman of Mrs. Fields Cookies to concentrate on the software business and eventually bought it from Mrs. Fields for $3.5 million. The system has been adapted by Burger King and Skipper's Seafood chains. Phar-Mor uses the payroll reporting system of Mrs. Fields Cookies and has agreed to install the cash, sales, and inventory reporting system that provides daily sales reports to management.

Then in March 1993, *Business Week* reported that Debbie Fields was "throwing in her apron," and stepping down as president and chief executive officer. While remaining "chairwoman" of the company, she "turned over nearly 80 percent of the company to four lenders led by Prudential Insurance Co."

Mrs. Fields Cookies illustrates a number of important IT design points. The company used electronic communications and electronic linking to coordinate headquarters and retail stores. Technology in the form of daily reporting systems made it possible for the store controller structure to be flat, a form of technological leveling. The example shows that you can use technology to personalize and control the business. All Mrs. Fields stores look alike.

Debbie Fields was very concerned about control and about quality; the technology helped her manage these two aspects of the business. As described in Chapter Two (Table 2.2), no single IT design variable substitutes for or supplements conventional control mechanisms. Mrs. Fields Cookies was able to combine IT and traditional design variables to create a structure to ensure control. First, the store controllers are a control mechanism. Second, the combination of in-store computers, uniform recipes and cooking instructions, and uniform ingredients provide quality control. Voice mail and e-mail also helped to motivate, and to some extent, to control employees. At Mrs. Fields, control comes from a combination of organization structure and technology.

But is IT to blame at Mrs. Fields Cookies? Did the use of nontraditional organization design strategies lead to Debbie Fields's giving up control of the business? Did the technology lead management into a false sense of confidence and invulnerability? Those questions are not yet answerable. It appears that Mrs. Fields Cookies became overconfident of its abilities to manage businesses that were not part of its core. A bakery and café chain is different from a cookie store chain. Technology allowed Debbie and Randy Fields to create different types of organization structures within the same firm. They could also "micromanage" what was happening at individual stores. The unanswered question is whether or not the technology helped lead top management away from the core business into ventures it did not understand well. Certainly this example illustrates that you have to manage all aspects of strategy and operations well; designing the world's best organization structure will not save your firm if its strategy or execution is fundamentally flawed.

Evolution of a Hybrid Organization at Frito-Lay

Another example of a well-known company that uses information technology in design is Frito-Lay, one of the leading snack food companies in the United States (this example draws from Applegate, 1993, and "Frito-Lay's Speedy Data Network," 1990). Frito-

Lay management made a major decision in the early 1980s to invest $40 million in a risky new project to develop handheld computers for the route salesforce.

Frito-Lay had about 10,000 routes at that time; each driver/sales representative called on a number of customers. Before the handheld computer, the job involved a lot of paperwork; sales representatives had to reconcile their cash accounts at home in the evening, and there were frequent disputes with the company. The new project was justified primarily on the belief that it would increase efficiency and provide more time for the route salesforce to actually sell the product. It was also expected to reduce "stales," merchandise that had to be discarded because it had not sold before losing its freshness.

The handheld computer had to be specially designed for Frito-Lay because there was no suitable device on the market at that time. The company also had to develop a satellite-based nationwide communications network to move the data from the sales offices to headquarters in Dallas. A large number of mainframe computer programs were modified, and computers were installed at the distribution centers to upload the data from the salesforce to corporate computers in Plano, Texas. The mainframe also downloads price changes and promotions to the handheld computers. On Monday, it sends each sales representative a review of the last week's result for his or her route. The network also permits e-mail, a further instance of electronic linking and communications.

The handheld computer allows the sales representative to scroll through the products that an account might order and indicate the quantities delivered. For the first time, Frito-Lay obtained data on exactly what its cash accounts were ordering; the accuracy of the records and the accounting functions meant that the sale representative did not have to spend hours reconciling receipts from the cash accounts. The system also reduced the need to take physical inventories and freed time for the sales representatives to provide better customer service.

The handheld computer improved operations at Frito-Lay; it also provided detailed information that had not been available before for cash accounts. With checkout scanners, grocery stores were developing better information on sales than manufacturers. The data collected on the handheld computers helped to give Frito-Lay comparable information.

Frito-Lay also developed the Executive Information System, a series of computer applications to facilitate management inquiries about sales. Given the new information, Frito-Lay management began a series of steps to change the way in which it handled marketing; the new concept is one of micromarketing. The company makes the data from the handheld computers available in a large database; regional sales managers can make queries of that database that tell them in great detail what products were selling at what stores. They can get reports on individual accounts for each brand and package size by type of store. A manager can find the answer to the question, "How many bags of Fritos were sold at the Seven-Eleven on Morris Avenue in Summit, New Jersey, last week?" The manager can also see pricing moves by competitors.

With this kind of information available, Frito-Lay no longer has to depend on national advertising campaigns; it can target advertising to the local market and anticipate its effects. The collection of detailed data on sales and the availability of that data in a database enabled this new marketing strategy.

There has been little publicity about the impact of the new technology on the structure of the organization, although Frito-Lay has laid off a number of managers. It is likely that this is a case of technological leveling. When increased data are made available to both lower and senior levels of management, there is no role left for managers who used to gather and summarize data for different levels of management.

A firm needs a strategy before it designs its structure. Frito-Lay is a good example of a strategy changing the way the organization is structured and how it operates. The Frito-Lay strategy was enabled by IT, and then the technology supported changes in structure. Decision-making power moved upward to senior management and downward to division managers.

Approaching the T-Form at Calyx & Corolla

The innovative organization Calyx & Corolla (first introduced in Chapter Two) was formed by an entrepreneur named Ruth Owades (this example is based upon Brokaw, 1993, and "In the Mailbox, Roses and Profits," 1992). Before starting C&C, Owades had successfully introduced a new distribution channel for gardening products when she founded Gardener's Eden, a mail-order business for gardening tools and accessories. After a few years, she sold Gardener's Eden to Williams-Sonoma and operated it for over four years as a division of that company.

Four years later, after careful and painstaking research, Owades decided to launch Calyx & Corolla. She had observed how inefficient the flower and plant market was in the United States. U.S. flower and plant sales run to $10 billion annually, with a substantial proportion of the flowers imported from countries like Columbia and the Netherlands. The distribution channel to retail florists is lengthy and involves a number of parties. Typically, a grower sends flowers to distributors in its growing region. From there, the flowers go to various wholesalers who distribute the product to florists, supermarkets, and other retailers (see the top diagram in Figure 7.1).

Owades's insight was that she could dramatically reengineer this distribution process if she could negotiate agreements with growers to prepare standardized floral arrangements and with a carrier to deliver flowers directly to the consumer. She wanted to eliminate all of the steps and organizations between the grower and the consumer (see the bottom diagram in Figure 7.1). While the idea was appealing, there were many in the industry who thought it impossible.

Figure 7.1. Models of Floral Distribution.

Traditional Floral Distribution

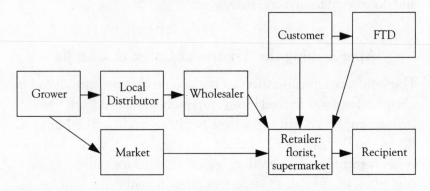

Calyx & Corolla Floral Distribution

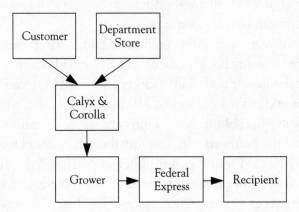

Owades, a master salesperson, worked with growers, encouraging them to experiment with her. One acquaintance, Peter Barr at Sunbay Growers, entered a test with Owades in which they tried shipping flowers, in different kinds of packages, via retail carriers. The experiment showed that it was feasible to package flowers for this kind of shipment.

Owades knew that she needed two things to be credible with parties who might provide financing. The first was a group of growers willing to make floral arrangements and package flowers for delivery to the end customer, a new role for the grower. A number of growers responded positively to her approach because they were looking for additional distribution channels and were sensitive to increasing foreign competition. Owades's second need was a first-class overnight delivery firm to lend credibility to her new business. She worked assiduously to penetrate management at Federal Express and interest the company in the concept. At that time, FedEx was campaigning for more mail-order delivery business, and eventually, it agreed to deliver flowers for Calyx & Corolla. To finalize the deal, Owades had to guarantee that she would cover losses from packages left without a signature.

Given growers and Federal Express, Owades now needed to interest the consumer in buying flowers by mail order. She hired as her management team several managers who had worked with her in the past, and together, they decided that the best way to inter-est the consumer was with an upscale catalogue that contained appealing photos of arrangements and plants along with informa-tion about the flowers and plants. The catalogue had to be inter-esting reading. By 1991, Calyx & Corolla was mailing over twelve million catalogues annually.

The final component needed to make Calyx & Corolla work was information technology. The entire concept depends on elec-tronic linking and communications between customers, C&C, growers, and Federal Express. Staff located in a San Francisco sub-urb answer calls on an 800-number and charge merchandise to callers' credit cards. Several times a day, C&C transmits orders via modem or fax to growers. Each grower has appointed a C&C account manager to supervise order printing, the selection and packing of flowers, the writing of gift messages, and preparation of FedEx shipping papers.

Federal Express picks up the orders at the end of the day and delivers the flowers the next morning anyplace in the continental United States. C&C must maintain a computer system to process orders and to select orders for transmission to growers based on the customer's desired delivery date. It must also handle accounting and make remittances to the growers and Federal Express. Finally, it must submit its credit card receipts to the appropriate card-processing company.

Earlier, I called Calyx & Corolla an example of a negotiated organization; it approaches the T-Form organization of the future. C&C by itself is relatively small. However, it has a number of virtual components, including a production and inventory facility (the grower), a highly computerized logistics and delivery system (Federal Express), an accounts receivable operation (credit card companies), and a large salesforce (the catalog). Clearly, the company uses electronic linking and communications, and there is a major electronic workflow from the customer to the order-processing group to the grower.

C&C also is a relatively flat organization, due to its negotiated agreements and compact management structure. Information technology plays a major role in making this kind of organization possible. It is the case with C&C as with Mrs. Fields that a new kind of organization was created. Of course, it is far easier to use technology and nontraditional designs when starting from scratch than when trying to change an existing organization. These two companies were also relatively small; it has been a considerable effort and expense to bring change at the much larger Frito-Lay.

Implications

Table 7.1 shows each of the IT design variables discussed in this chapter and its contribution to the three firms described here. Two of these firms have used IT design variables to create a unique organization structure that differs from traditional organization designs (Mrs. Fields Cookies and C&C) or have changed its structure to some extent as a result of technology (Frito-Lay). While these variables make possible a large number of structures, I suggest that the greatest advantage will come from using them to create a T-form organization.

Table 7.1. IT Design Variables and Organization Structure.

IT Design Variable	Example
Electronic linking and communications	Frito-Lay, with salesforce and with management; Mrs. Fields, between headquarters and the stores; Calyx & Corolla, between headquarters and growers
Technological leveling	Mrs. Fields, store controllers; Frito-Lay, management
Virtual components	Calyx & Corolla, for production, inventory, distribution, and sales
Electronic workflows	Calyx & Corolla, flow of orders from customer through order entry to growers

This chapter also shows how IT design variables affect the entire organization and how they contribute to the T-Form structure. *Electronic linking and communications* and *technological leveling* help give the T-Form organization a flat structure and encourage the delegation of tasks and decentralization of decision making. *Electronic workflows* provide employees with the information they need to make decisions. *Virtual components* are a way of providing customer service and of making a company more efficient; they encourage strategic alliances.

Recommended Readings

Applegate, L. "The Frito-Lay Consolidated." Case study. Boston: Harvard Business School, 1993.

Brokaw, L. "Twenty-Eight Steps to a Strategic Alliance." *Inc.*, Apr. 1993, pp. 96–104.

"Frito-Lay's Speedy Data Network." *The New York Times*, Nov. 8, 1990.

"In the Mailbox, Roses and Profits." *The New York Times*, Feb. 14, 1992.

Ostrofsky, K. "Mrs. Fields Cookies." Case study. Boston: Harvard Business School, 1988.

Chapter Eight

Information-Based Operations: New Ways to Do Business

Organizations exist to accomplish some goal, often to make a product or deliver a service. *Operations* refers to the processes involved in creating that output. Information technology has had a dramatic impact on operations, and this chapter shows how the IT design variables of *electronic customer/supplier relationships, electronic linking and communications, virtual components,* and *production automation* play a role in structuring operations.

Electronic Linking Through EDI

A typical order-processing cycle is inefficient when communications are by voice or by mail. As we saw in Chapter Five, a customer generates an order through a purchasing system, a purchasing clerk enters the appropriate data and prints an order to be mailed to a supplier, the supplier keys the order into an order entry system, and keying continues as both the customer and supplier reenter the same information in their respective computer systems. Electronic data integration (EDI) networks as one response to the inefficiencies in the order-processing cycle will be discussed in Chapter Eleven. Here we will consider how a firm gets started with EDI. What motivates trading partners to enter into an EDI relationship?

In some industries, trade associations have sponsored EDI or groups of firms have joined together to create systems. With broad industry support, it is easier for individual firms to develop standards and to justify their investment. But how does an individual company go about this process? And what impact might

EDI have on the firm? Reynolds Aluminum Supply Company offers an example.

In the late 1980s, Reynolds Aluminum Supply Company (RASCO) investigated the potential of electronic data integration for its operations (this example draws upon Boynton, 1990). RASCO is one of twelve divisions of Reynolds Metals Company, the second largest aluminum producer in the United States. At the time, RASCO operated twenty-four branches that served about forty states; it was represented in most parts of the United States except the upper Midwest. RASCO was the nation's largest distributor of aluminum mill products and the second largest distributor of stainless steel mill products, though its market share for each product was less than 10 percent. Its raw materials went into the manufacture of such varied items as highway signs, automobiles, commercial kitchen equipment, hospital equipment, aircraft, aluminum siding, and wine vats.

RASCO's strategy was to create a large service center network specializing in aluminum, stainless steel, and nickel-alloy products. The company had specific market share objectives. In addition, over the years, RASCO had increased shipments by 60 percent while reducing its number of employees by 12 percent. It had also solved its high turnover problem, with the average employee having twelve years of service, up from five a decade before. One of RASCO's key operating measures is inventory turnover, that is, how many times a year the inventory is sold and replenished. The company's objective was to reach five turns a year.

RASCO was concerned with the direction in which the industry was moving. Customers were becoming interested in just-in-time production (discussed in more detail later in this chapter), which would require an EDI link. RASCO also wanted to reduce its own ordering overhead with suppliers, so EDI had an appeal for Rasco's communications with both suppliers and customers.

The company faced a number of problems in deciding how to get into electronic data integration. First, it recognized the asymmetrical relationship it had with suppliers and customers. On the one hand, it could ask a lot from suppliers; they wanted to continue doing business with RASCO. On the other hand, customers had alternatives to doing business with RASCO, and while some were very interested in EDI, others were not. It is hard to force a customer to do something; rather, you have to be responsive to customer demands.

RASCO also faced the problem of exactly how to set up EDI links. Since the United States has no national EDI infrastructure and RASCO's industry was not heavily involved in planning for EDI, the company itself had to choose a course of action. RASCO chose a multifaceted strategy. It began its effort by experimenting with Allegheny Ludlum, one of its biggest suppliers. RASCO and Allegheny had as many as twenty-five transactions with each other every day, which shows the potential for EDI to have an impact. Then, expanding its EDI efforts, RASCO encouraged suppliers to adopt the ANSI X.12 EDI standard; it also offered this option to customers who were capable of using X.12. For others, RASCO could install a PC with a proprietary link to RASCO's order entry system, or a customer could go through a third-party value-added network such as General Electric Information Services Company (GEISCO). With this flexible strategy, RASCO was able to create electronic links to all types of suppliers and customers.

While organizations today have a great deal of interest in EDI, we still have a long way to go in creating a completely linked electronic economy. However, more and more firms are receiving "letter bombs," announcements that state that the company has to support EDI links or lose the business of the company sending the letter. R.J. Reynolds recently sent such letters to 1,500 vendors who represent 10 percent of its trading partners. However, these 1,500 vendors receive 11,000 orders a year from Reynolds at an average order-processing cost (not merchandise cost!) of $75. The company figures that the cost of an EDI order is $0.93 (*Datamation*, 1993, p. 15).

In addition to their usefulness in manufacturing, EDI-like connections are of great interest to service organizations that process large amounts of data. The insurance industry, for example, is moving to standardize some of its existing electronic transactions. Because standards in the field were not developed, there are about 400 different electronic data formats used to transmit medical claims. Given the focus on medical expenses in the United States, improving the claims process would help reduce the estimated 24 percent of the U.S. health care budget that is spent on administration.

Applied to operations, EDI ultimately affects organization structure. It should improve efficiency and reduce costs, probably reducing the need for clerical employees. It is basic to establishing electronic customer/supplier relationships and represents a form of electronic linking and communications. As we shall see below, it is also important in creating certain kinds of virtual components in the production process.

EDI is fairly simple in concept, but it can be very difficult to implement. The ANSI X.12 standard is a help, but it allows a large number of variations to suit individual needs; these variations tend to defeat the purpose of a standard. Also, companies should be aware that most EDI today is a form of batch processing; the orders are not sent in real time. Rather, the receiving firm must check its input queue of electronic orders. It then processes those that have arrived. Yet even with this first generation of EDI, the trend is clear: firms will continue to link themselves with trading partners electronically. Firms that fail to adopt this technology will have a distinct disadvantage. First, they will lose business as customers insist on dealing only with those who can communicate electronically. Second, firms that cannot communicate electronically will suffer a significant cost disadvantage.

Lean Production

One of the reasons that electronic data integration is very popular is the movement toward lean production and just-in-time (JIT) inventory. While these two concepts are often described as synonymous, JIT is only one part of lean production. Lean production begins with a different concept of the factory than typical mass-production manufacturing (Womack, Jones, and Roos, 1990). In a lean production facility, space is kept to a minimum to facilitate communications among workers. You see very few indirect workers like quality control inspectors, people who add little value to the final product. And you are likely to find only a few hour's worth of inventory at each production station.

If a worker finds a defective part, he or she might tag it and send the part to a quality control area to receive a replacement part. Each worker is probably able to pull a cord to stop the assembly line if there is a problem, yet the focus is on solving problems in advance.

When developing new products, a lean firm is likely to use matrix management and design teams. The chief designer of the Honda Accord, for example, "borrowed" people from appropriate departments for the duration of the project. Key decisions are made early in design, and the team is not afraid of conflict. Because manufacturing representatives are included on the design team, an effort is made to see that the new product can be manufactured efficiently.

A key aspect of lean production is coordinating the supply chain. For example, a modern automobile contains some 10,000 parts, many of which come from outside suppliers. In a lean auto plant, over 70 percent of the components are likely to be purchased from external vendors. In the Japanese auto industry, the strategy is to establish long-term relationships with these suppliers. The automaker helps the supplier improve production and quality; savings are split between automaker and supplier. What the automaker gives up in terms of choosing from competing suppliers is made up by getting dependable and high-quality parts from the chosen suppliers.

The most important component of lean production, however, is management and its beliefs about how the firm should operate. The GM-Toyota experiment known as the NUMI plant, located in Fremont, California, shows clearly how management's beliefs and attitudes affect innovation. The idea of the joint venture was that GM would learn lean production techniques from Toyota; Toyota was in overall charge of the plant, and various GM managers were a part of the management team. The plant, using rather limited automation, achieved better production results on a number of measures than plants GM was heavily automating at the time. But in spite of the clear benefits of lean production, it was resisted throughout the rest of GM, contributing to the ongoing crisis at the world's largest automaker. Lean production worked at NUMI, but GM management's attitude hindered its adoption in the rest of the company.

Lean Production and JIT at Chrysler

An excellent example of lean production and just-in-time inventory comes from Chrysler, a firm that has come back from the dead at least twice in the last twenty years (this example is based on Addonizio, 1992). Chrysler committed itself to lean production; it already was close to Toyota in the number of parts purchased externally, about 70 percent compared to GM's 30 percent. Lean production at Chrysler means working with some 1,600 external suppliers who ship materials to fourteen car and truck assembly plants in North America.

Key to lean production and JIT inventory is EDI. In the early 1990s, Chrysler had some seventeen million transactions per year with suppliers. The automaker implemented lean production in 1984, and by 1990, it had reduced overall on-hand inventory from five days to forty-eight hours, eliminating more than $1 billion from its inventories.

Chrysler also followed the model for lean production set by the Japanese. It studied components and options and redesigned them to reduce complexity. Engineers worked with suppliers to be sure parts were packaged so that they would not be damaged in transit; there was little buffer inventory to make up for a bad part. The marketing staff developed forecasts to stabilize schedules for the assembly line. A stable build schedule is important for suppliers so they know what goods to deliver and when to send them. Chrysler moved to in-sequence building. A car begins the production process in a sequence in relation to other cars and stays in that position until finished; people do not pull a car off the assembly line for special work. This practice provides predictability for parts suppliers and lowers transactions costs.

To further reduce transactions costs, Chrysler has begun a pay-as-built program with some suppliers. In this program, Chrysler counts the number of cars built each day and computes the number of a vendor's parts in that car. Chrysler computers then wire payment to the vendor for the materials used during the day. If the company built 1,000 Jeeps with Firestone tires, it would pay Firestone for 5,000 tires (four plus a spare for each Jeep) for that day. The vendor does not have to bill Chrysler, and Chrysler has many fewer transactions to process.

Chrysler also took advantage of its JIT capabilities to reduce less-than-truckload (LTL) delivery costs by 15 percent (Harrington, 1990). From its predictable schedule for what is to be built, Chrysler developed scheduled pickup loops. A carrier now follows the same route each day, picking up from multiple locations. As a result, the LTL shipments are "consolidated." Much like a school bus driver, the same driver makes the same stops each day. This program is one of the methods that has allowed Chrysler to trim some in-plant inventories from two days to four to six hours.

The production process described here could not function without information technology. The production automation of manufacturing systems including forecasting, build plans, and materials requirements planning creates the kind of stable production and advance notice required for lean production and JIT to work. Because the flow of parts has very little room for error, communications to suppliers must be instantaneous. Electronic linking and communications and electronic customer/supplier relationships are key to making JIT work. These design variables also contribute to efficiency through, for example, the electronic linking of the pay-as-built program.

What has happened to Chrysler's inventory? Where has $1 billion worth of goods gone? Chrysler now has a virtual inventory. No longer stockpiled at Chrysler plants, the inventory exists at suppliers and is linked to Chrysler through an electronic network. This network informs suppliers when goods are needed, and they in turn respond. But do the suppliers have Chrysler's inventory in their warehouses? Probably not. If Chrysler provides a supplier with predictable demand, then each supplier can practice JIT with its suppliers all the way back through the value chain. Greater connectivity throughout the production system has driven out physical inventory and substituted electronic flows of information. Certainly IT alone is not enough; the companies involved have to make many other changes in their operations. However, the technology described here is a crucial enabler of lean production and JIT inventory.

Failure to Take Advantage of IT at ABZ

In many of the previous examples in this book, we have seen the importance of management in adopting IT-supported changes. What happens if management fails to manage information technology or to take advantage of the IT design variables? ABZ, a real company whose name has been disguised, illustrates what happens when management takes a disinterested approach to technology.

ABZ makes electronic components; it is a leader in its field with high quality and a wide product line. Production is complex, and the company's engineers have designed and built much of the company's manufacturing equipment. For at least a decade, however, the company has been ill-served by information technology. A succession of general managers has tried to improve computing and communications at the firm and then has lost interest owing to the difficulties encountered.

ABZ suffers from a number of problems. First, being located in a tourist area, it has few skilled IT professionals to draw upon. Second, management has never bothered to develop an understanding of what is required to create and manage useful applications. The company's IT group is a high-cost, low-payoff operation. Managers at ABZ did not view the IT group as a resource until recently.

During the last ten years, as ABZ's staff have seen what IT has done for customers and suppliers, much more enthusiasm for technology has arisen in the firm. However, the central IS group has had poor leadership and input from management; its systems do not seem to make a major contribution to moving the firm ahead.

After learning about companies who connected their customers to their order entry systems in the 1980s, ABZ developed a link to its system for its distributors. The effort took two years, and the system was not well received by the distributors. By that time, they were using more advanced systems from ABZ's competitors.

ABZ was not able to escape from EDI; its best customers were all more sophisticated than it was in the use of this technology. One of the company's major customers is a mail-order electronic components firm I will call WMS. While WMS sells to individuals, it does a great deal of business with industrial firms needing electronic components.

WMS has applied technology extensively to its operations in order to reduce costs and improve service. Its warehouse is highly automated and employs bar coding extensively. A computer screen tells the picker what to select for an order. Racks holding components move to the warehouse picker, much the same way a dry cleaners' storage rack operates. The picker reads the bar code on each parts bin with a wand, to verify correct selection of the ordered part. Items that fit in a standard box are packed by automatic machinery, weighed, and the proper United Parcel Service information is generated for payment purposes. One machine softly blows a printed delivery ticket with glue on its back onto each box.

WMS, given its reliance on technology, was an early adopter of EDI for its major suppliers like ABZ. WMS invested heavily in software programs that would map its orders to fit customer requirements, even though it was using the basic X.12 standard. It had a project manager and two programmers working full-time on EDI with its suppliers. ABZ struggled to adapt to the program, and with a great deal of help from WMS, did manage to link to this important customer.

The ABZ example does not demonstrate a great success story or the use of IT variables in organization design (except at WMS). What the story does illustrate is the importance of keeping up with and managing technology. It is impossible to use IT design variables if you have no confidence in your firm's technology. WMS is continually pushing the envelope of what can be done with IT while ABZ is always trying to catch up. Into which category does your firm fall?

Federal Express as a Virtual Component

In the partnerships that create virtual components, a firm must be willing to trust its partner, and the partner has to perform. Federal Express is a good example of a firm that is trying to partner with a number of companies.

We have seen, in Chapter Seven, the services it provides to Calyx & Corolla. Another example is the House of Windsor Collection, a British catalogue company that stocks all of its products at a Federal Express facility in Memphis. FedEx handles all packing, shipping, invoicing, and accounting for the London firm. The House of Windsor offers forty-eight hour delivery in the United States, courtesy of its partner. FedEx also downloads data from its computers that the House of Windsor uses to make its marketing, merchandising, and financial decisions. Federal Express is a virtual subsidiary in the United States for the House of Windsor.

Implications

This chapter has looked at IT in operations (Table 8.1 summarizes the IT design variables used by the companies discussed in the

Table 8.1. IT Design Variables and Operations.

IT Design Variables	Example
Electronic customer/supplier relationships	RASCO, EDI; Chrysler, EDI, scheduling, pay as built; WMS, EDI
Electronic linking and communications	RASCO, EDI; Chrysler, EDI, scheduling, pay as built; WMS, EDI; FedEx and the House of Windsor Collection
Production automation	Chrysler, lean production and JIT; WMS, warehouse operations
Virtual components	Chrysler, supplier inventory; FedEx and the House of Windsor Collection

chapter). Through networks, these companies have made progress toward the goal of electronic integration. Through *electronic customer/supplier relationships*, they are eliminating paper and the inefficient rekeying of information from one company's system into another's.

Through lean production and JIT, these companies have created *virtual components*, with dramatic reductions in inventory. More than just inventory reduction, lean production is a kind of automation that uses *electronic linking and communications* rather than automated equipment to improve production. Lean production should make it possible to reduce overhead and shrink middle management.

IT variables that help design operations are aimed directly at improving the production of goods and/or services. All of them are important for the T-Form organization, which must be both efficient and effective in its operations. The IT design variables used in the companies described here have made a major contribution to operations, enabling the firms to drive costs out of the production process while also improving quality. It is in these ways that IT will contribute to the internal operations of the T-Form organization, providing it with many of the advantages it holds over the conventional firm.

Recommended Readings

Addonizio, M. "Chrysler Corporation: JIT and EDI (A)." Case study. Boston: Harvard Business School, 1992.

Boynton, A. "RASCO: The EDI Initiative." Case study. Charlottesville, Va.: Darden Graduate Business School Foundation, 1990.

Harrington, L. "Driving Down Inbound Costs." *Traffic Management*, Nov. 1990, pp. 43–48.

Chapter Nine

Customer-Based Service: A New Focus for Business

One of the corporate strategies discussed in Chapter One was focusing on customer service: the customer is put in first place; employees provide service beyond what is expected and what the competition offers; plans and programs are developed to improve service to customers. Dell Computer, for example, has built a large technical support staff that provides free consultation over an 800-number; Dell mentions its "award winning" service staff in advertisements for its products. This chapter discusses firms that have used technology in implementing a service-oriented corporate strategy. It focuses on the IT design variables of *electronic linking and communications, electronic customer/supplier relationships,* and *virtual components.*

It is easy to say that a firm will be focused on the customer, but it is much more difficult to create that emphasis on the part of employees. The technology to be described here can help by providing systems and connections to customers, but management must also instill the belief in employees that customer service is important. One approach to motivating employees in this direction is to alter the organization's reward structure and compensate employees for providing outstanding customer service. Compensation practice is a traditional organization design variable that is a very important tool for management in shaping the organization.

David Kearns, for example, has written about his extensive, long-term effort to change the corporate culture at Xerox when he became chairman of that company (Kearns and Nadler, 1992). He found Xerox to be an arrogant company, paying attention to its own products and not to the needs of its customers. He feared that Xerox might not survive as a company owing to the serious flaws he saw in its approach to business. The number one problem was its lack of attention to product quality, an important part of customer service.

Kearns started a multiyear, ultimately successful effort to involve the entire workforce in a program to increase quality and focus on the customer, and one of his tools was to base compensation partially on customer satisfaction. At one point, Xerox was sending out 50,000 surveys a month to customers to gauge their satisfaction with Xerox products and services. This is an example to bear in mind, while studying the following applications of IT to customer service.

Customer Service at Otis France

Customer service can take many forms. Otis Elevator of France is one example of a company that has developed a number of technology-based programs to improve customer service (this example is based partly on Loebbecke and Jelassi's 1992 study of this United Technology subsidiary's approach to business). Otis France has over 6,000 employees to service about 40,000 customers; the company has a 40 percent market share. There are two aspects to its elevator business: sales and service. While sales are important, they tend to be cyclical. The service business is more profitable and more consistent; elevators must be serviced regardless of the condition of the economy. Sales generate outright revenue and also lead to service contracts; some 60 to 80 percent of new customers buy service contracts from the manufacturer of their newly installed elevators.

One of the methods Otis France is using to give customers better service is Otisline, a competitive use of information technology developed by another Otis division, Otis North America, in the mid 1980s. Otisline is focused on customer service in the repair business. The system maintains a complete maintenance record on each customer's elevator. When a service call is received at the service center, Otis representatives use the system to dispatch a repairperson and to record the results of the repair call. This dispatching feature means that a repairperson can respond quickly to a problem and can get information about the repair history of an elevator. In addition, Otis maintains a great database, showing possible problems with its products or maintenance. In one instance, an elevator of a particular model had an excessive number of service calls (well above average for the model) in one part of Florida. Because the database identified the unusual number of calls, Otis North America was able to immediately dispatch the person who knew most about that model to investigate and rectify the problem.

In France, Otisline is offered as a service for which customers are charged. Customers to the service can dial a toll-free number to reach dispatchers who then send a repair person. The system receives 2,400 calls a day from customers and 800 calls a day from Otis service staff.

Otis France has also been successful in selling the concept of remote elevator monitoring (REM). This feature, developed by Otis North America for worldwide sale, can be built into an elevator, using a computer chip that monitors the elevator's performance and that dials Otis on a dedicated telephone line if the elevator is malfunctioning. The idea is to dispatch a repairperson and fix the elevator before the customer even realizes there is a problem. While REM did not attract customers in North America, Loebbecke and Jelassi report that Otis France has 7,000 elevators using the system.

Otisline is an example of electronic linking. One can envision modifications at some point in the future that would allow the customer to access Otisline and its database directly rather than through a human intermediary. REM is an example of such a direct link; it shows that electronic customer/supplier relationships can be completely automatic under certain conditions.

Customer Service at Picker International

Picker International, headquartered in Cleveland, sells medical diagnostic systems (this example draws upon Wallace, 1994). It has long had a good reputation for the quality of its field service, which is handled by a group of some 900 engineers. Before Picker developed new technology to support its field force, each field engineer had to be equipped with a pager, test equipment, and a car full of three-ring binders stuffed with parts catalogs, schematic diagrams of equipment, and other documentation for the firm's products.

For a number of years, Picker has used a packaged program running on a mainframe computer for field service dispatching. Over the years, Picker has modified this program to support its business; the system handles dispatching, keeps records of calls and inventory, and bills customers. Once, field engineers interacted with the dispatchers through the telephone; after being paged they called the dispatcher for instructions. At the completion of the repair, the engineer called the dispatcher to describe the repair, the parts replaced, and customer information, all of which was entered into the system. Management uses such data to measure the quality of field service and to study product reliability. The company tracks equipment performance, mean time to repair, the speed of response to customers, and other indicators of service quality.

Picker management realized that it needed to overhaul its support system for field engineers if it was going to continue to offer high-quality customer service. Its equipment was becoming increasingly complex, and many of its products now have dial-in capabilities that allow an engineer to test and diagnose equipment remotely. Therefore, the decision was made to equip the field engineers with laptop computers and software to support access to remote databases. It was also necessary to modify the mainframe dispatching system. The complete project required an investment of about $2.5 million.

With the laptops and a PC interface to the mainframe, engineers now log on to the central computer when they are paged rather than calling the dispatch center. An engineer can view all open service calls and can download the past service history for each call to the laptop. This information has always existed in the mainframe, but until they had PCs, engineers could not access it. The engineer also logs information about the repair. Now that the field engineers enter these data, Picker has been able to reduce the number of people in the dispatch center and reduce input errors.

To further improve the repair process, Picker developed an expert system to assist the field engineers. Each engineer has access to on-line documentation that incorporates diagnostic steps developed by experts at Picker on each piece of equipment. The laptop program leads the field engineer through the steps in diagnosis and displays product information on the screen.

The investment in time to develop the expert system was high; the development of the knowledge base just for Picker's computed tomography product line required three months and some three hundred hours of work by the systems designer. The laptop has documentation that is linked through hypertext; selecting a highlighted word or phrase takes the user to a piece of documentation that explains the selected text in more detail. The documentation includes text, diagrams, figures, and product schematics.

As a result of these efforts, the field engineers have access to the company's accumulated knowledge about each product. They are estimated to be 40 percent more productive with this system, and this means that customer equipment is out of service for less time. Picker has successfully used electronic linking and communications with its field repair staff to provide better service for customers; it will increasingly provide electronic links with its products installed at customer sites in order to offer remote diagnosis and possibly even repair.

Customer Service Through an Electronic Market

Our next example of customer service comes from England. Chapter Five discussed the impact of the "Big Bang" on the London Stock Exchange. Changes in securities regulations resulted in a major upheaval in the stock market, with benefits going primarily to customers. The new environment for securities trading encouraged competition and the creation of electronic markets, markets we call virtual when compared with the old trading floor.

Clemons and Weber (1991) have studied this new market with emphasis on the electronic system developed by Barclays de Zoete Wedd (BZW). BZW was created through purchases and mergers that brought together Barclays Merchant Bank; Barclays Investment Management subsidiaries; de Zoete & Bevan, a U.K. broker; and the jobber (broker) Wedd Durlacher Mordaunt & Co. In 1988, BZW began offering its electronic system TRADE, which is used by brokers to execute customers' orders. The system has reduced trading costs for customers and doubled BZW's share of small orders. One of the factors responsible for TRADE's success is that BZW has chosen to be a market-maker in over 1,800 equities, of which 1,400 are available electronically through TRADE. The system places orders at the best available price at the time of the trade, it routes buy and sell orders to the market-maker at BZW covering the stock, and the trade is automatically reflected in the market-maker's book of shares. The trade is confirmed for the customer in a few seconds.

A broker calls TRADE from a PC with a modem in his or her office. BZW installs the software without charge, software that also sends trade and settlement information to other computers in the broker's office. The system has three main functions including the capture of order data, the automated execution and confirmation of trades, and the routing of settlement information. The broker receives a quote that is valid for thirty seconds; he or she trades by entering the quantity of shares to buy or sell. One advantage of the system is that the broker only needs to enter data once; the system routes settlement information to the broker's settlement service, either a contractor or an in-house system, depending upon the original input from the broker.

Here, electronic linking and communications result in an automated trade, lower costs, and better customer service in the form of speed and accuracy. In particular, Clemons and Weber point out these four advantages to TRADE:

1. The system promises the best execution for the customer. The trade takes place at the highest bid and the lowest offer quotes posted by any of the competing market-makers.

2. The system increases the speed of execution; brokers do not have to make separate telephone calls to market-makers to execute a transaction. The end-customer has a better chance of obtaining the best price under this system, especially during times of rapid price movements.

3. The system lowers trading costs for the customer.

4. The system provides the broker with more flexibility; he or she has another channel besides the telephone for reaching the market-maker. In fact, TRADE transactions take place over a private packet-switching network, so the broker can still execute transactions even if there are problems with the voice telephone system.

The TRADE system has also created a number of advantages for BZW. The first, of course, is increased market share in small trades. The system also lowers BZW's costs for executing small trades. Because the system keeps an accurate accounting of the market-maker's book, or inventory, he or she is aware of the company's position in the security. The system also helps reduce unmatched trades and errors in trades.

TRADE is not alone; the London Stock Exchange offers its similar SAEF system, and Kleinwort Benson Securities has its BEST system. However, SAEF in 1991 was only processing about 10 percent of the combined volume of TRADE and BEST. Of the three systems, TRADE is by far the most successful. The reason appears to be the large universe of stocks that the system includes, almost the entire set of stocks traded on the London market. By making a market, and committing the necessary capital, for 1,400 stocks, BZW provides outstanding customer service. TRADE has substituted electronic linking and a virtual electronic market for a physical stock exchange.

Electronic Customizing at Levi's

A firm can also use technology to serve the retail customer directly. Levi Strauss is rolling out a system in its Original Levi's stores that allows women to order custom-fitted blue jeans (Rifkin, 1994). A salesclerk measures the customer, using instructions from a computer as an aid. The clerk enters the measurements, using a touch screen, and makes adjustments to the data based on the customer's reaction to various sample jeans she has tried on.

The store PC relays the final measurements to the subcontractor who developed the system; this firm sends the measurements electronically to a fabric-cutting machine at the factory. Factory workers attach bar codes to the cut pieces to track them as they make their way through the manufacturing process. At the end of assembly, scanning equipment sorts the custom jeans and routes them for a Federal Express delivery. The total elapsed time is about 2.5 weeks for a custom pair of jeans. In the first store using the system, Levi's found a 300 percent increase in jeans sales over the same period the previous year. Electronic linking has provided a new level of service for Levi's customers and appears likely to increase Levi's market share.

Electronic Customizing at Panasonic

Levi's is not alone in using technology for custom manufacturing. Another example is the Panasonic Corporation in Japan, which offers customers semi-customized bicycles priced midway between mass-produced and totally customized bikes (Bell, 1993). Customers have a limited choice of options (over eleven million different combinations) compared to a fully customized bike. A buyer chooses among ten styles of frame and from fifteen sizes of either chrome-molybdenum or chromoly steel and thirteen sizes of either aluminum or carbon fiber. He or she can specify one of three head angles for the front fork, one of six variations in the stem for the handlebars, one of four handlebar widths, and one of two gearing choices. The buyer also gets to choose among 191 color schemes.

The local bike shop takes the customer's order and faxes it to the factory for input into a CAD/CAM system that generates drawings to test the design and a bar code number for all components. A veteran craftsman is responsible for each bicycle; he works beside robots that perform routine chores. Measuring systems check the custom-made frames to determine if they are acceptable. A host computer directs the spray painting machines according to instructions called up by the bike's bar code. The computer also indicates which of the set of possible components (such as gears) the customer has chosen, by lighting up the storage station containing each component part for this bicycle. The factory produces an average of fifty to sixty personalized bikes a day and requires eight to ten days to build a bicycle, about twice the time a mass-produced bike requires. The personalized bike is about four times the cost of a mass-produced one, but only about half the price of a totally customized bicycle.

In the United States this kind of production is being called *agile manufacturing*. The objective of the movement to agile manufacturing is to serve customers better by allowing the customer to input custom or semi-custom orders directly into the supplier's computer. Linking customers and suppliers together will improve customer service and flexibility and will reduce cycle times. All of this is made possible through electronic linking and communications.

Defensive Strategy at McKesson

Adopting customer service as a strategy is appealing to an increasing number of firms. No longer does one sell a product alone; the product comes with a package of services that the customer has come to expect. For McKesson Drugs, customer service became a defensive strategy to preserve its sales. McKesson is a wholesale drug supplier, and its customers are independent drug stores. In 1974, the wholesale drug industry was fragmented, with 180 or more distributors competing for more than 50,000 customers. The major threat on the horizon was the drugstore chain. The chains featured central purchasing and distribution; they could buy in quantity and resupply their stores economically. As the large drug chains grew, McKesson's customers were forced out of business, and the firm faced a dramatic loss of sales.

The distribution system for independent druggists was also highly inefficient; McKesson had over 100 regional warehouses with the stocked items laid out in alphabetical order by name. Customer orders were filled in random sequence, resulting in a lot of wasted effort as pickers moved back and forth through the warehouse.

By the mid 1980s, the structure of the industry had changed to one of much greater concentration. Now there were only 90 wholesale distributors, half as many as a decade earlier. Market share for the largest distributors had increased significantly. The independent drugstores, the customers for McKesson, had decreased in number from 40,000 to 34,000, and their market share had dropped from 58 percent to 40 percent.

In the early 1970s, McKesson had began the development of Economost, an electronic order entry system for drugstores. Clemons and Row (1988) have documented McKesson's motivation for creating this system and its subsequent development and results. McKesson wanted to reduce its costs and tie its customers more closely to its distribution business since, at the time, it was not unusual for a druggist to order from two or three distributors on the same day. However, McKesson had a more unusual reason for developing its system; it feared the demise of its customers and therefore its market. The threat of the drug chains was very real; the independent druggist needed help in competing against these chains. McKesson could help the independents by making them more efficient and by providing goods at a cost that would be competitive with the chains. The Economost system, then, was designed as an offensive strategy for providing customer service and

tying customers to McKesson and as a defensive strategy for pre-
serving customers.

Economost allows customers to enter orders electronically with
the wholesaler. The druggist walks through the store with a handheld order entry device and indicates what goods should be
reordered. Some druggists use a bar-code scanner to capture the
identification of an item to be ordered, others use a McKesson
seven-digit identifier that they key into the handheld computer.
When the druggist has finished, he or she sends the order over a
toll-free line to the McKesson national data center in California.

The same day or one day later, McKesson delivers the items.
The new stock comes in cartons that match the druggist's aisle
arrangement so that he or she does not have to sort cartons or
goods. Shelves are restocked with a single pass through the store,
just as the order was entered. The druggist also receives price stick-
ers that he or she can customize to obtain different margins and to
reflect manufacturer's discounts and similar promotions. McKesson
estimates that it provides over 93 percent of over-the-counter goods
and 99 percent of pharmaceuticals the next day.

One drugstore reported to Clemons and Row that restocking
alone used to require one clerk full-time; with Economost, ordering and restocking take about a half day each. The system has created a virtual inventory, as this druggist now carries no stock beyond
what is on the shelf, except for special promotions.

McKesson also provides services beyond the order entry features
of Economost. The druggist can purchase a number of reports based
on the business the pharmacy does with McKesson, reports that
show inventory, goods with advertising allowances, and similar out-
puts. McKesson also provides third-party claims processing to
encourage pharmacy customers to keep coming back to a store that
is supplied by McKesson. The druggist submits claims on customers'
insured prescriptions to McKesson, which pays the druggist the
insurance amounts. Then McKesson handles submitting the claim
to the insurer.

It is difficult to determine the impact of a system over a multi-year period. Clemons and Row (1988) estimate that since 1975, McKesson has invested between $20 million and $30 million in Economost. The company has about forty information systems staff members devoted to the system. However, McKesson has reduced the number of order entry clerks from 700 to 15 since electronic ordering began, and the warehouse staff have enjoyed annual productivity increases of 17 percent from 1975 to 1985. McKesson now has a larger share of its customers' business. From 1975 to 1987, McKesson's sales increased 424 percent, from $922 million to over $4.8 billion. At the same time, operating expenses increased 86 percent. However, McKesson does not appear to have earned substantial excess profits; its performance matches closely its largest competitor, which has developed similar systems.

What does appear from this analysis is that through a program that involves electronic linking and communications and electronic customer/supplier relations, McKesson has implemented an offensive and defensive strategy of providing the best customer service possible. This strategy has helped increase its market share, and more important, has helped prevent the company's customer base from disappearing.

Implications

The companies discussed in this chapter have all used IT design variables to implement a strategy of customer service (the variables are summarized in Table 9.1). *Electronic linking and communications* are important in connecting customers and their suppliers; the speed of this kind of communication makes it possible for organizations to be very responsive, developing strong *electronic customer/supplier relationships*. *Virtual markets and inventories* can also greatly improve what is offered to customers.

A technology-based approach to customer service appears to create a competitive advantage. The companies described here

Table 9.1. IT Design Variables and Customer Service.

IT Design Variables	Example
Electronic linking and communications	Otisline, service order entry and service force management; Picker, links to field force; BZW, linking brokers to market-makers; McKesson, linking drug store customers to its distribution system; Levi's and Panasonic, linking factories and customers
Electronic customer/supplier relationships	Otisline, service order entry and remote elevator monitoring; Picker, connection to field engineers and customer equipment; BZW, broker link; McKesson, multiple links and services to customers; Levi's and Panasonic, custom-ordering systems
Virtual components	BZW, electronic market; McKesson, virtual inventory for druggist

seem secure in their industries despite threats from strong competition. In many instances, the benefits from the firms' investments in technology appear to have accrued primarily to their customers. However, this result is an expected outcome of a customer-oriented strategy. By focusing on the customer, a firm develops a stronger customer base, which, in turn, enhances its competitive position.

The T-Form organization is designed to excel at customer service. The purpose of electronic customer/supplier relationships and frequently of virtual components is to improve the quality, responsiveness, and efficiency of the T-Form firm's interaction with its partners. High-quality operations (discussed in Chapter Eight) combined with outstanding customer service will provide the T-Form organization of the twenty-first century with a strong competitive advantage.

Recommended Readings

Clemons, E., and Row, M. "McKesson Drug Co.: Case Study of a Strategic Information System." *JMIS*, Summer 1988, pp. 36–50.

Clemons, E., and Weber, B. "Barclays de Zoete Wedd's TRADE: Evaluating the Competitive Impact of a Strategic Information System." Working Paper no. 89–03–08, The Wharton School, University of Pennsylvania, 1991.

Loebbecke, C., and Jelassi, T. *Staying at the Top with Otis Elevator: Sustaining a Competitive Advantage Through IT.* Fontainebleau, France: INSEAD, 1992.

Wallace, S. "Experts in the Field." *Byte*, Oct. 1994, pp. 86–96.

Chapter Ten

Group-Based Communications: Changing the Way We Manage

This chapter examines the IT design variables of *technological leveling*, *electronic linking and communications*, *technological matrixing*, and *electronic workflows* as they apply to members of management themselves. One of the most difficult questions to answer about organizations is, what do managers do? For the first three or four decades of information technology availability, IT did little to help managers in their day-to-day tasks, often because IT staff did not understand managers. There were not very many true *management information systems*, though many companies claimed to have them. The last five years, however, have witnessed the development of IT groupware and IT group meeting rooms that are aimed at supporting the daily, mundane tasks of management. But what are these tasks?

Over twenty years ago, Henry Mintzberg (1973) conducted a classic study of top managers, observing their behavior by living with them for a week. As a result, he was able to identify a number of roles that a senior manager plays in an organization. One of Mintzberg's roles of management that seems to be universally agreed upon is leadership: the manager is and should be a leader for the organization. In this role, the manager sets direction, acts as a public spokesperson, and tries to see that the resources of the organization are employed to achieve the objectives he or she has set forth.

Management researchers have emphasized the decision-making nature of management since the 1950s. A number of academics suggest that the most promising focus for the study of management is the decision. Certainly, we expect managers to make important decisions in many different domains, such as R&D funding, product development, and new product introduction. Many managerial decisions revolve around issues of resource allocation; almost every organization is confronted with limited resources and competing demands for them.

In addition to the leadership and decision-making roles, a third role that managers often face is that of disturbance handler; disputes and problems in the organization find their way to the manager who is in a position to resolve them. These disturbances may come from inside the firm, or they may be prompted by problems with suppliers or customers.

Managers also deal with information in their jobs; they function as spokespeople for their firms. A good manager scans the environment for competitive actions, threats, and new opportunities. Today, companies can be strongly affected by certain external influences, such as government regulations and actions. The terms of trade treaties, for instance, can make a major difference to a firm's strategy and operations.

These are a manager's roles, but what does a manager actually do during the day? Mintzberg divided the tasks he observed into five categories. The first category was scheduled meetings, which consumed over half of the day for the CEOs he studied. Next came unspecified desk work. Unscheduled meetings took 10 percent of the day, while telephone calls consumed 6 percent of managers' time. Finally, managers spent a small amount of time on "tours," that is, management by walking around.

This distribution of time begins to get at the daily tasks managers perform. More important, cutting across all the roles and all the tasks are two activities: communication and information processing. As a leader, spokesperson, decision maker, and disturbance handler and in most other roles, the manager is communicating with others. He or she disseminates the strategy and goals of the firm. He or she receives communications from subordinates, customers, suppliers, the financial community, and many others. Meetings, both scheduled and unscheduled, involve communication, as do phone calls and tours. Much desk work involves letters and memos, another form of communication.

Many communications and much purposeful managerial work revolve around information processing. We frequently communicate to obtain new information. When making a decision, the manager must process information to determine the appropriate course of action to take. Suppliers and customers want information. The securities industry seeks information about company plans and performance.

Thus, it appears that managers spend a great deal of time communicating and dealing with information. They publish and consume large amounts of information. They use this information in a variety of ways to make decisions, allocate resources, and see that members of the organization work toward achieving its goals.

As we saw earlier (Chapter Two), the Leavitt model of the organizational framework includes *people* and *tasks* along with technology and structure. So far, we have been looking primarily at the technology and structure and processes. Now it is time to turn to the people and tasks. *The technology described below is designed to support people in the organization in the tasks they are expected to perform.* It lets managers and other workers redesign their tasks, and it provides a great deal of flexibility and a number of alternatives for the flow of work, communications, and coordination.

Information Technology and Groupware

Groupware is an exciting and relatively new technology that is aimed at helping managers in what they do. Most information systems prior to the development of groupware were oriented toward solving such organizational problems as how much of a product to produce, how to process orders, and so on. Groupware is aimed at what a manager does; it *supports members of the organization who have a common task and who operate in a shared environment.*

Groupware is sometimes called coordination software because

it helps managers coordinate the work of others in the firm. By such coordination, managers mean to assure that the resources of the firm are applied to achieving its objectives. Coordination means managing dependencies, that is, seeing that individuals or groups who depend on each other or on common resources function effectively.

In the other sections of this book, I have not found it necessary to discuss a specific software product, but in describing groupware, it is difficult not to focus on Lotus Notes, a product that has about a three-year head start on the competition. At the beginning of 1995, Lotus Notes had an installed base of nearly four thousand companies and more than one million users around the world. For many people today, groupware and Lotus Notes are synonymous. There are competing products, but as yet, they lack the features of Notes. Microsoft has included some components of groupware in Windows for Workgroups, and Novell is also building groupware into some of its applications.

What is groupware? Even the vendors have difficulty describing the nature of these flexible products. Generally speaking, however, Notes is based on the emerging model of client-server computing. The product assumes that users, or clients, are connected on a local area network with a server. Databases to be shared are kept on the server, though people may also have local databases on their own PCs. Notes helps users manage this shared database. Thus, one major feature of Lotus Notes is its ability to replicate databases across departments and organizations. You can tell Notes how often to synchronize databases, and it will make sure that all information is consistent.

For example, suppose that you work for an advertising company and that teams in the New York and Rome offices are preparing a campaign for a global client and using Notes as they work. The system could be set up to automatically update databases at, say, 9:00 P.M. Eastern standard time. Notes will update both the New York and the Rome databases, adding new information without losing existing data. Thus, team members in New York and Rome can make changes during the day with impunity; the software replicates those changes on both copies of the database. If people in two locations change the same information, Notes flags it for them to resolve.

The database replication feature is one of the coordination features of Notes. The software coordinates diverse workgroups and allows them to share information without having to worry about updating it. Just having the same database easily available to multiple individuals working on a project, regardless of replication, promotes coordination as well. Notes also has its own e-mail system so that Notes users can communicate with each other.

Another feature of Notes that makes it suitable for supporting individuals who have a common task is its applications development tools. It is fairly easy to design quite powerful applications and share them. For example, it took me and some colleagues about fifteen minutes to design a shared database of the common materials (videotapes, computer demonstrations, and so on) available for each class session of an M.B.A. course in information systems.

Groupware at a Consulting Firm

How are businesses using Lotus Notes? Significant users of the system include General Motors Europe, major consulting firms, and several Big Six accounting firms, including Peat Marwick and Coopers & Lybrand (Kirkpatrick, 1994). When we studied how one consulting firm used the technology, we found that, interestingly enough, Notes was not used extensively to manage customer engagements. Rather, the firm was using Notes internally to improve administration.

Just like any other company, a consulting firm has to administer itself. This firm, with revenues in excess of one billion dollars a year, has to administer personnel, manage billings and collections, administer contracts, and perform a wide variety of administrative tasks. The practice manager for the Northeast described how Notes improved his operations. With the help of this groupware, the firm had developed a number of administrative applications, and his group of direct reports from around the region had been able to reduce the number of their meetings dramatically.

Compaq Computer has found that its sales staff uses Notes to communicate with customers and that salespeople now rarely come into the office, preferring to work at home. Boston Market (formerly, Boston Chicken) is growing at 100 percent a year; it uses Notes to keep track of expansion plans, market research, advertising, cooking procedures, and recipes. Essentially, the firm's groupware is becoming the leading dispenser of knowledge in the corporation.

Groupware at Chase Manhattan Bank

Chase Manhattan Bank is another major Notes site, with over 2,700 users across a highly distributed network. One of Chase's major applications is a service that follows investment reports from providers like Dow Jones. The system is designed to help the analyst spot differences between the bank's evaluation of a company and the evaluation from these other services. Explanations about the differences are posted to a Notes database, where they are widely available.

The chief information officer at Chase feels that Notes is unique because it lets people develop applications that they would not previously have undertaken. That is, the applications are easy enough to construct that systems ideas that would have been infeasible using older technologies, suddenly become easy to justify. Chase is using Notes in its systems development division on a variety of projects. It is particularly useful in coordinating employees across company locations in Brooklyn; Lexington, Massachusetts; and London.

Groupware at Chemical Bank

Lynda Applegate and Donna Stoddard (1993) have reported on the use of Notes at Chemical Bank. At Chemical, it was the corporate systems division (CSD) that first became interested in groupware. The senior vice president of CSD was launching a productivity program to generate more output from the design and programming staff at the bank. He felt that the division's work was communications intensive and that the division was breaking down as it used conventional forms of communicating. His estimate was that Notes would allow a 15 percent productivity improvement for a staff whose salaries totaled $15 million a year. He also viewed a test in CSD as a good preview for rolling Notes out in the rest of the bank.

The bank brought in a groupware consultant and offered training in the use of Notes in anticipation of the implementation. The vice president hired a full-time Notes specialist and formed a Notes support group to assist users. Rollout began with twenty senior managers and their secretaries. In a period of less than two years, 300 CSD employees were using Notes, and they had developed more than ninety applications for the bank with Notes.

In the middle of this effort, Chemical decided to centralize IT resources and then to initiate a 40 percent reduction in IT staff. Shortly thereafter, Chemical Bank announced its merger with Manufacturer's Hanover Bank. During this period, turmoil ruled the systems division; therefore, one major application the vice president initiated was the "rumor mill." Employees who were concerned could post rumors to the rumor mill database, and senior managers would respond. The vice president felt that this simple technique had helped create a feeling of trust and openness in the group.

One manager remarked that Notes let developers create applications quickly to respond to specific business needs. It also helped create geographical independence: for example, in one application, a group in New York worked with developers at a Texas bank owned by Chemical. Groupware let the teams coordinate development and work together despite their physical separation. Notes also makes group work largely independent of time since it reduces the need for face-to-face communications.

Examples of some Notes applications at Chemical include the following (Applegate and Stoddard, 1993):

Top Staff Discussion is a database of progress status reports. Instead of discussing project status at their meetings, individual top staff members post that information in the Notes database for others to read. Staff meetings now focus on more complex problems and decisions.

A broadcast news application provides a bulletin board on which the entire CSD worker community can post items of interest.

A teller application involves a database of changes needed and implemented for a mainframe system to support branch tellers as a single point of service to retail customers. Members of the project team that developed the application reported to different managers and worked at various bank sites. Notes helped to overcome the different affiliations and locations of team members. The leaders of the project used Notes to share project status, obtain information more efficiently, and discuss decisions without having to schedule frequent meetings.

Impact of Groupware

In late 1993, the *Wall Street Journal* had an article about groupware and its impact on organizations; the staff writer found that groupware tended to erode organizational hierarchies (Wilke, 1993). In some cases, however, groupware has also created problems for management. The Chemical Bank vice president discussed above resigned after the Manufacturer's Hanover merger, and his successor eliminated the rumor mill. It seemed that the forum became "unruly" and began to receive a number of cutting criticisms of management. The thrust of the *WSJ* report, however, was more positive. The reporter talked to various managers who felt that groupware was helping them dissolve corporate hierarchy by making it easy to share information. The rank and file can join discussions with senior management if given access to groupware.

One major contribution of groupware is making organizational intelligence available where it is needed. A worldwide consulting firm with thousands of employees has a great deal of expertise. If a consultant in Japan needs to find out if the company has solved a problem similar to the one she is facing in some other country; groupware can provide this base of intelligence.

A related benefit of groupware is the way shared information can be used to enhance decision making. This technology may make it easier to create decision-support systems and expert systems by making data and expertise widely available in an organization.

A number of companies are using Notes to connect electronically with clients and suppliers. In 1995, Lotus and AT&T began offering a system called Network Notes. In this system, AT&T provides public servers that offer users a version of Notes software, making it easy to establish electronic connections among firms that employ Notes. Officials at Lotus present Network Notes as the "defining element of the Information Superhighway," feeling that electronic commerce is far more important than video on demand or games.

Of course, there are a few cautions needed. Like the telephone system or any other network, Notes and Network Notes work only if everyone who needs to be involved has access. Networks only become useful to service providers and consumers when they reach a critical mass. Some observers feel that groupware could be used to increase rather than decrease authoritarian tendencies in a manager. However, it is hard to see how groupware would provide any benefits if the information it contains were to be restricted to a privileged few.

Orlikowski and Gash (1993) have found what may be a more serious problem with groupware. She studied the use of Notes at a major consulting firm and found that the product did not achieve its potential. Her belief is that the firm rewarded its staff members for individual behavior, not for their contributions as a group. A staff member got ahead because he or she had specialized knowledge and skills that could be sold to a client. Groupware encouraged staff to share this knowledge, but doing so would result in the loss of an individual's competitive edge. It is clear from this analysis that the norms and reward structure of an organization may have to change if it is to take advantage of tools like groupware.

Group Meeting Rooms

Another system that some experts classify as groupware is the meeting support system (see Vogel and others, 1988–1989). This type of groupware requires that the needed people get together in one place—a specially designed meeting room. A frequent design employs a U-shaped table so that individuals can see everyone participating in the meeting. Each position at the table has a personal computer connected to a local area network. The meeting is then supported by various types of software and generally involves a facilitator.

The meeting is likely to start with a brainstorming session. Here, the facilitator will ask people to focus on the topic of the meeting and generate and enter as many ideas as possible. Idea analyzer software accepts inputs from all participants and displays the comments on each person's PC anonymously; each person can see all comments but does not know who made each one.

The next step might be to use the software to analyze the issues or to group the comments into categories for analysis. Other software might help people rank issues and/or solutions to the problems discussed; this kind of groupware is likely to include some kind of voting tool, so that participants can vote on the ideas they consider the most important.

The last piece of basic software is a policy formulation tool that can help the group develop a policy statement or solution from the meeting. Beyond these basic pieces of software, some meeting room systems include advanced functions. The group facilitator might use a questionnaire tool to design an on-line questionnaire for collecting data from participants. Software to support stakeholder analysis can help evaluate the implications of a proposed plan of action.

Electronic meeting rooms have stimulated extensive research, especially in business schools, but the results of the research are mixed; many results consist of anecdotes and testimonials. At least one large company built many electronic meeting rooms after using the prototype room at the University of Arizona. Participants in these electronic meetings seem enthusiastic about the results. However, one drawback may be the rather large number of ideas that can surface in a short period of time; there have been reports of hundreds of ideas coming from a half-hour brainstorming session. Voting on or ranking these ideas is a formidable task.

An electronic meeting with anonymity in discussion is certainly a threat to the authoritarian manager. Do managers really want the creative ideas of subordinates? What if these ideas differ from the managers'? By its anonymous nature, a meeting in an electronic meeting room provides a degree of leveling. It is not hard to imagine distributed electronic meeting systems in which individuals in different places could all be on-line at one time or in which they join conferences, all anonymously. This kind of communication should tend to reduce the need for multiple levels of management, further leveling the firm.

Implications

Groupware is a technology designed to support *people* and the *tasks* they perform in organizations. It encourages users to build applications to improve their productivity; it also facilitates communications, a major task for most workers today. In addition, groupware, and to some extent electronic meeting rooms, can be used to implement some of the IT design variables we have been discussing.

Groupware is relatively new, and its impact is not completely clear yet (Table 10.1 summarizes the IT design variables and groupware used in the firms mentioned in this chapter). First, it appears to

Table 10.1. IT Design Variables and Groupware to Support Managerial Tasks.

IT Design Variable	Example
Electronic linking and communications	Chase Manhattan Bank, linking 2,700 users across the bank; Chemical Bank, linking CSD employees to each other and management; AT&T Network Notes, linking multiple companies.
Technological leveling	Potential suggested by observers, not seen yet in companies surveyed; electronic meeting rooms and their possible extension help level the organization through granting anonymity.
Technological matrixing	Chase Manhattan Bank, developers in diverse locations work on projects; Chemical Bank teller application and joint group working on project in New York and Texas.

have the potential to create matrixed workgroups with some ease. The technology facilitates the sharing of information across different locations and time zones. Groupware should encourage *technological matrixing* and make it easy for management to set up temporary task forces, monitor their work, and dissolve them when their work is done.

Second, groupware has the potential to reduce the number of layers in an organization. In many organizations, layers of management exist to request input from the next lower layer and pass it along to the next highest layer. There is little need for such managers when a network and groupware make information readily available across the organization. We saw earlier that managers spend a great deal of time communicating and soliciting information. Groupware enhances communications channels in an organization so that, again, the organization needs fewer people to process information. As a result, it seems predictable that groupware products will encourage *technological leveling*. As discussed above, electronic meeting rooms may also contribute toward leveling.

Some firms are also using Lotus Notes for *electronic workflows*. Here, information that requires different people to process it in some order is routed and its completion overseen through groupware procedures. This chapter does not have an example of such an application, but it is certainly feasible, given the capabilities of current groupware products and their add-ons. Organizations are also establishing *electronic customer/supplier relationships* in which groupware allows customers and suppliers to share organizational databases.

Groupware is a very exciting technology, and we are just discovering how to exploit it. The dominant implementation strategy is to convince managers that the products will help the company so that the managers distribute them to users. These users are then asked to be creative in developing interesting applications. This implementation model suggests that the technology is becoming democratized and that authoritarian hierarchical management will have a short future in a groupware environment.

Thus, groupware addresses the people and the internal operations of the T-Form firm. It will provide a repository of organizational intelligence, a database that helps individuals at all levels access the information they need to make decisions without having to rely on a managerial hierarchy. It will facilitate the use of internal communications and especially *technological matrixing* to solve problems quickly using the minimum number of people possible. In the long-term, it is expected that groupware will flatten the organization, a key characteristic of the T-Form structure.

Recommended Readings

Applegate, L., and Stoddard, D. "Chemical Bank: Technology Support for Cooperative Work." Case study. Boston: Harvard Business School Publishing, 1993.

Vogel, D. R., and others. "Electronic Meeting System Experience." *JMIS*, Winter 1988–1989.

Part Four

Building the
Technology Infrastructure

Information technology design variables depend on the existence of an information technology infrastructure. To better understand the building of a technology infrastructure, consider this nation's transportation infrastructure. Interstate highways, airports, and railroads are examples of that transportation infrastructure. Each of these components has been subsidized at one time or another by the federal government. A single state does not have the revenue nor the incentive to create superhighways in its state alone. The interstate system developed when there was a national plan for highways connecting each state along with federal funding for constructing those highways.

Similarly, each department in your company may be able to justify a local area network, but it is unlikely that each one of them could develop its own international network. However, the company as a whole might develop a worldwide voice and data network, so that it is available to the various departments when they need it. This global network would be the center of the firm's technology infrastructure.

Companies frequently require individual applications of technology to be cost justified, but infrastructure expenses are difficult for any one individual or group to justify. Because a technology infrastructure, especially in the form of communications networks, is so important to the T-Form organization, I devote the two chapters in this part of *The T-Form Organization* to that subject. Much of what is discussed here requires corporate investment to facilitate the use of IT design variables in building a T-Form organization.

Chapter Eleven discusses the exponentially growing world of networks. Not only are individual companies investing in global networks, but groups of companies have formed alliances to interconnect themselves electronically. The United States is also debating the merits of a national network infrastructure to advance education and commerce. Chapter Twelve looks at the technology beyond networking that is required for the T-Form organization. The technology needed to use IT design variables *already exists*. But in order to use those variables to create the T-Form organization, a firm has to develop a robust technological infrastructure.

Chapter Eleven

Networks: The Ubiquitous Electronic Alliance

Electronic linking and communications, virtual components, technological leveling, electronic workflows, technological matrixing, and *electronic customer/supplier relationships*—almost all of the information technology organization design variables that are crucial to creating a T-Form organization depend on communications and networks. A network consists of a series of computers or other devices connected by communications links. Networking is the fastest growing part of information technology, though this rapid growth has led to many alternatives and much confusion. This chapter examines the networks currently available and the multifaceted roles networking can take in an organization's business.

The Impact of Communications Technology

Our existing telephone system is a good place to start an examination of communications networks. This large international network has a number of important features. First, it is ubiquitous, at least in the United States where almost all residences have telephone service. Even though there are different phone companies, they all interoperate, that is, a call from a regional Bell company can be made transparently to a telephone in a GT&E company. Through the work of international standards organizations, telephones also interoperate at the country level. You can direct dial telephones in a large number of foreign countries.

The existing U.S. telephone network is constantly being upgraded; higher speeds and higher capacity links are having a dramatic affect on life in some parts of the country, especially in rural areas. Some 400 rural counties where population dropped during the 1980s are now growing; 900,000 people moved to rural counties during 1990 and 1991. To revive its rural areas, Nebraska state officials pushed local telephone companies to install fiber-optic lines and digital switches. The carriers laid 6,700 miles of fiber-optic lines, linking all but five of the state's counties.

The impact of this new network has been dramatic. During the 1980s, Aurora, Nebraska, with a population of 3,800, had over twelve empty storefronts and the population was shrinking. Today the unemployment rate is less than 1.5 percent and all the stores are occupied. An Aurora pet food plant uses the updated telephone network to link to its headquarters in Ohio and with shippers and customers around the country. The company has said that a decade ago, communications would not have been on its top ten list of reasons to locate a plant in a particular place; today it is in the top three.

One small high school in a town of 135 people uses the network for interactive television classes in Spanish since the school is not able to justify a language teacher. Students in the Spanish classes use a fax machine for written work. Ainsworth, Nebraska, has a two-way videoconferencing unit in the town library. Recently, senior citizens used the system to discuss arthritis with nurses in Omaha.

For the T-Form organization, networks of computers and other devices are a key element of technology. The most familiar computer connection in organizations is to a local area network (LAN). A LAN connects computers within a small geographical area like a building or a floor of a building. In a typical LAN, computers can communicate with each other and with a server, a computer that contains programs and data to be shared among all users. For a network that must extend over greater physical distances, a wide area network (WAN) is configured. A WAN might be used to connect LANs in two different cities.

One of the nicest attributes of the telephone network is simply the fact it is already there; we have a communications infrastructure that makes it simple to plug a new telephone or fax into the network. We can buy a telephone from a number of different sources and know that it will function on the network because there are published standards and vendors manufacture their equipment to meet these standards.

Building Networks

Developing computer networks is not as easy; there is no single infrastructure for data comparable to the telephone network for voice. Of course, we can simply use modems and dial-up voice lines, but for many applications this alternative is either too costly or infeasible because the existing voice lines are comparatively slow at transmitting data other than voice messages.

In the United States, companies have typically developed two different kinds of networks: electronic data interchange (EDI) using standard protocols and/or proprietary data networks. In private industry and government, EDI has become extremely popular for lowering costs while increasing accuracy and quality in purchasing goods. As discussed earlier, the objective of EDI is to reduce manual keying, reduce errors, and speed up the order cycle. By exchanging data electronically, organizations can change their production cycles and the kinds of services they offer.

Despite their achievements, EDI networks have had less impact than one would expect because firms cannot rely upon a common telecommunications infrastructure. Given the lack of a data network infrastructure in the United States, firms face a bewildering number of choices when considering the development of a network application. As a result, to use EDI effectively takes expertise and resources. Applications are expensive to develop since there is much reinvention with each new network. For companies to exchange data, they must completely agree on data formats. A firm sending a purchase order must put data in exactly the right place in the electronic message so that the supplier can interpret it. The high cost of initiating networking gives larger firms an advantage over smaller competitors in using data networks.

The ANSI X.12 standard is intended to facilitate the EDI process, but a number of industry-specific networks do not conform to the standard. Some press reports have indicated that, due to incompatibilities, up to 50 percent of the data exchanged via EDI needs rekeying. Firms might have to change their internal computing systems or purchase special software to map the data from existing systems to an accepted EDI standard. While some service companies can help a firm get started, and PC EDI packages are available for smaller firms, the start-up and maintenance costs are too high for many companies. It is also hard to get all trading partners to use EDI. Generally, it is the larger firms that are more sophisticated technologically that can afford the development cost.

It is to alleviate such problems that a group of fifty Northern California companies has created a consortium called Commerce-Net. The objectives of this ambitious project are to allow companies that have never done business with each other before to establish and maintain a relationship electronically. CommerceNet plans to use the existing Internet as its underlying network. It must develop agreements on standards for proposals, bids, price lists, and other transactions. The idea is that a company, say, in Palo Alto, could put out a request for proposals in the morning and receive bids from respondents all over the world by evening. The next morning, it could send an electronic purchase order to the winner. AT&T, Novell, and Lotus are also working together to allow companies to link Notes and NetWare networks more easily, a technique that would offer another possibility for electronic commerce.

Partially because U.S. firms cannot rely on a national data infrastructure, they have developed elaborate private or proprietary networks, sometimes using common carrier facilities, and at other times bypassing them completely. Examples of familiar companies using proprietary networks include Federal Express and United Parcel for package delivery, United and American Airlines for reservations, Frito-Lay for distribution and decision support, Baxter Healthcare for supplying its customers, and many other firms we encounter on a regular basis.

Each of these firms has to bear the expense of designing, implementing, and operating a proprietary network. Some of these efforts even required inventing new technology. Frito-Lay undertook the development of a handheld computer for its drivers to use for placing orders and keeping records. United Parcel developed a network that features cellular data communications from its trucks to UPS computers. If a firm operates in an industry in which there is no support for or tradition of EDI, today it has little choice but to develop a proprietary data network for an application or use a service company's existing network.

A National Network Infrastructure: Minitel

There are two examples of national and international networks that offer a great deal of promise for creating conditions to encourage the T-form organization: the Teletel, or Minitel, system in France and the Internet system, which is based in the United States. The French Teletel system, popularly called Minitel after the name of its first terminal, was introduced in 1982 by France Telecom, the French government-sponsored telecommunications company (the Minitel example is based partly upon Lucas, Kraut, Streeter, and Levecq, 1995). By 1993, Minitel was used in 20 percent of households and 80 percent of businesses in France; users access a wide array of communication, information, and business transaction services. Approximately 6.5 million Minitel terminals are in service in France, which has a population of 57.5 million. Another 500,000 residents of France use Minitel on their personal computers. Altogether, about 40 percent of the nonretired French population has access to Minitel either at work or at home. Some 23,200 services are available on the system, a number that has been growing at the rate of 10 percent a year, with no signs of a slowdown.

Minitel is the first and only example of a successful mass market network venture in the world. It is successful in the sense that it reaches a large proportion of French households and businesses; it offers a rich variety of information, communications, and services; and it is estimated to be profitable. Mass market services in the United States, like Prodigy, Compuserve, Genie, and America On-line, were relatively unsuccessful at first, though they have been growing of late. For the most part, these U.S. services fail to offer much opportunity for businesses.

In 1989, Minitel introduced a nationwide electronic mail system for businesses and the general public. Information services include the national on-line telephone directory and schedules for the French national railroad, as well as want ads, stock market reports, and other information that might be found in a newspaper. There are also short-lived or highly specialized information services for the general public. For example, sports fans can access continuously updated information about the position of boats in around-the-world yacht races, and parents sending their children to camp can access daily lunch menus.

Because Minitel was built on a nationwide data network with open standards, businesses also make use of the network for business-to-business services. While Minitel began with a mass market focus, in recent years residential growth has slowed and been replaced by a large growth in business applications; in 1990, about half of the services were business related. Some of these business services are traditional information services, with data such as stock market listings, economic information, or airline schedules tailored to the interests of business customers. Other business applications are business-to-business transaction services, very similar to EDI and proprietary network applications in the United States. Braun Passot, the second largest office product supply company in France, encourages its customers to order electronically via Minitel. For large volume customers, however, Braun Passot installs a computer with a proprietary connection to its order-processing and reporting system.

A number of case studies conducted by Charles Steinfield at Michigan State University illustrate what can be done with a network that connects businesses to small firms and consumers. A large multinational electrical appliance and consumer electronics manufacturer used Minitel for EDI-like connections to approximately 10,000 separate retailers and independent repair people throughout France. In addition to the major cost savings this manufacturer was able to achieve by better managing inventory and reducing transactions costs, the firm also was also able to introduce a revenue-producing expert system–based training application that assists the service force in the diagnosis and repair of appliances and electronics products. Repair staff are charged on the basis of connect time for use of this service. In addition, the expert system accumulates data on repair problems and provides feedback to the design and manufacturing divisions of the company in order to help them detect and correct potential structural flaws in their products.

Minitel's ubiquity enables other innovative business applications as well. In one, a clothing manufacturer has been able to use the Minitel terminals already in many boutiques to offer custom-tailored suits. A clerk takes a customer's measurements, ships them over Minitel to a computer-controlled cutting machine at the manufacturer's factory, and the factory returns a custom-made suit in several weeks. Another application is the trucking spot market created by Lamy, the French directory publisher. Freight forwarders transmit special shipment requests to a Minitel database that truckers search as they attempt to fill excess capacity or to find a cargo for a return trip. Upon finding a matching offer, the truckers immediately call the forwarder to make a bid.

Discussions with French firms suggest that, using Minitel, it is possible to develop a national order entry system in several months for well under $50,000, something very difficult to accomplish in the United States if you must build a proprietary network for the application.

The Amazing Internet

While Minitel shows one way that a national data network can succeed, as a result of a centralized governmental telecommunications policy, the Internet provides a decentralized model of a government-subsidized network. The Internet is a worldwide interconnected collection of computer networks, started in 1969 as the Arpanet, a military-sponsored research project on how to build reliable networks in the face of unreliable components. But over time, as additional research laboratories, universities, and even personal computer networks became connected to it, the Internet became an infrastructure for scientific and educational computing in the United States and in a significant portion of the world.

It is clear neither who owns the Internet nor who controls it. While the National Science Foundation (NSF) originally subsidized the Internet, costs today are shared by the largest users (universities, research and development companies, and government laboratories). In addition, these institutions supply labor in the form of highly paid professionals to maintain and upgrade the network. Institutions pay a flat rate to join the Internet, and individuals in these organizations do not pay any fees. External access providers generally charge a flat rate to connect to the network, in the range of $20 per month.

While it is not known with any certainty how many users there are, 1995 estimates are that there are over two million computers and probably over thirty million users worldwide. Recent estimates are that the Internet is growing at the rate of a million users a month. Between 1991 and 1994, traffic on the Internet doubled annually. While scientists and engineers were early users, followed by academics, today the Internet is available to commercial firms and to the general public. Since 1992, over 50 percent of the networks newly connected to the Internet are in the commercial domain.

The Arpanet was originally designed so that scientists and others could conduct research on computer networking itself and gain access to remote computers and files. Within months of the opening of the Arpanet, however, interpersonal communication in the form of electronic mail and computerized bulletin boards became the dominant application. Today, there are approximately 8,000 bulletin boards distributed across the Internet. On-line real-time conferences, in which users join a group and chat by passing text messages back and forth, are becoming increasingly popular. There are also various multiuser games for recreation.

Today on the Internet, we find a huge variety of applications and information sources. In Philadelphia, the Internet was used to provide reading-improvement courses over the Internet to 100 low-income homes equipped with PCs for the test. No one signed up for reading-improvement classes when they were offered in the schools, but students and some parents eagerly registered when given the opportunity to use borrowed computers in the safety and privacy of their own homes. The Internet Talk Radio Show provides news and entertainment to users with audio software and speakers on their workstations. An NSF-sponsored project at New York University is making the Securities and Exchange Commission EDGAR database of corporate findings available on the Internet. In May 1994, one could find current weather maps for any region of the country, an on-line exhibit of items from the Vatican Library, artwork from several museums, the complete Grateful Dead lyrics, and photos of model Cindy Crawford, to name just a small set of services.

The Internet can now be used for profit-making applications as long as one does not use the network backbone subsidized by the National Science Foundation, although there is a great deal of confusion over what is acceptable use. A number of independent service providers make it possible for a company to access the Internet and avoid the NSF backbone. Government agencies, for example, post requests for proposals to Internet servers, and contractors can file their bids electronically. There are also a number of job postings available, and companies including AT&T list information about themselves. Mead Data Central provides Internet access to its Lexis/Nexis database on a subscription basis.

The Internet is also used extensively to share and distribute software. Through anonymous FTP (file transfer protocol), a user can log on to a remote computer as a user with the name "anonymous," use his or her Internet address as a password, and transfer files from the remote computer to a local computer over the network. Dell distributes new versions of its software via the Internet as well as through other channels.

The Internet has been criticized for its difficulty of use; however, gopher servers, the World Wide Web, wide area information servers (WAISs), and the Mosaic interface are making the network easier to use. Anyone with an Internet address can download free gopher server and client software to set up an information resource. Many universities have created gophers that contain a hierarchical directory to information about various aspects of the school, for example, registration, general information, financial aid, libraries, schools, degrees, and the like. Anyone on the Internet with a gopher client program can access this information. One publishing firm has placed abstracts of all its products on a gopher server.

Wide area information servers provide a distributed text-searching mechanism. Every document in a WAIS database must be indexed by contents, something done automatically by WAIS software. A user then can enter text and the WAIS software will identify the documents in a database containing that text. A public domain version of WAIS can be used with gophers to provide this search capability.

Researchers at CERN (European Organization for Nuclear Research) in Geneva developed the World Wide Web (WWW), which connects an estimated 30,000 network servers. The web uses hypertext links produced with the Hypertext Markup Language (HTML) to link documents and files, so that certain words in a text reference other sections of text or other documents. Clicking on a highlighted piece of text with a computer mouse retrieves a related file or document, allowing the user to browse through related pieces of information. The retrieved documents may all reside on different computers, but the WWW makes all retrieval transparent to the user.

Users of the WWW need an appropriate interface program; Mosaic, developed at the University of Illinois at Urbana, is a popular choice to access the WWW and other Internet resources. Many people feel Mosaic is responsible for some of the recent growth in Internet use. This program works by pointing and clicking with a mouse, which is a vast improvement over character-based terminal access to the Internet. Mosaic connects users to different services, helping them to navigate around the confusing and disorganized structure of the Internet. It can also create forms and facilitate the publication of data. While not yet close to providing the kind of development environment for service providers that Minitel offers, Mosaic is moving the Internet in the direction of greater ease of use.

In short, open standards have helped the Internet to grow and have enabled many people and organizations to become information providers and many users and service providers to connect. The World Wide Web, gopher servers, Mosaic, and WAISs all operate across many different types of platforms and make the network interface far more pleasant than it once was. The network has an open, decentralized, and extendible architecture, and its open culture and free exchange of software have also encouraged users and providers. A spate of articles (and occasionally cartoons) on the information superhighway, "cyberspace," and the Internet have made network connections highly fashionable. All of these factors have led to the critical mass needed for Internet to succeed.

Networks, the IRS, and New Business

Networks facilitate the development of new kinds of business, business that uses the network to implement IT design variables. Kambil and Short (1994), for example, have studied the impact of electronic filing on the tax preparation industry, an example that illustrates some of the benefits that accrue from networks.

In 1990, the Internal Revenue Service (IRS) began an electronic tax return filing program nationwide. Return preparers or filers authorized by the IRS can transmit individual returns to the IRS electronically. The system returns a receipt, and the filer can arrange for a direct deposit of any refund. This system has the potential eventually to affect one hundred million individual taxpayers. Some seventy-five million of these payers receive an average refund check of $900.

About forty million people use professional tax preparation services. H&R Block has over a third of this market and is considered a commodity preparer. There are also individual or small CPA firms and large accounting firms that do tax preparation work. Finally, there are investment services firms who prepare returns for high-income individuals.

The Internal Revenue Service's electronic filing initiative has created new roles in the tax preparation industry: electronic filers, communications network providers, software vendors, and consumer credit providers, to name a few. One example of a new business initiative promoted by electronic filing is the instant refund in the form of a refund anticipation loan to the electronic filer from a credit provider. When the electronic return is transmitted, the IRS checks its accuracy. Given this verification, the credit provider issues a loan against the security of the anticipated IRS refund. The tax return can even mandate that the refund go directly to the credit provider. One New York bank offers a three- to five-day no-interest refund advance along with electronic filing to its customers for a $45 fee.

In addition, electronic filing is forming other electronic relationships in the financial industry. Information on a tax return, gathered by the tax preparer, can be communicated to a tax planner; the planner can then create a customized investment portfolio to reduce future tax liabilities. The portfolio recommendations can then be sent electronically to an investment broker.

Another possibility enabled by electronically linking the tax preparer with the IRS is that a retailer could provide consumer credit through an instant refund linked to a store credit card. The retailer, in partnership with a tax preparer, might arrange for a discount on tax preparation or for store discounts if the refund is directed to the customer's store credit card account.

Thus, the networking initiative by the IRS, undertaken to improve its capabilities for processing returns, has created new opportunities for a variety of businesses. It has encouraged electronic linking and communications among those involved in tax preparation and related financial services and electronic customer/supplier relations (the IRS considers us to be its "customers").

Proprietary Networks: EDS

Proprietary networks also illustrate the specific benefits of networks to businesses. EDS has supplied an estimated 50,000 networks to its customers; this services firm takes responsibility for setting up the network and for operating it if the customer so wishes. EDS's own network, EDSNet, is the world's largest corporate data network; the company has an estimated $1 billion invested in it. EDSNet links 500,000 workstations and terminals, ninety-five data centers containing 142 mainframe computers, and 15,000 satellite dishes in thirty countries. The net handles over fifty million transactions a day and has a storage capacity of nearly fifty trillion pieces of data.

EDSNet helped EDS reduce its own layers of management through technological leveling; in 1989, the company reduced the levels between the customer and the chief executive from seven to three, in the process forming thirty-eight autonomous business units. EDS uses its network to form virtual task forces for bidding on contracts; the entire resources of the firm can be made available to any business unit. The network can also be used to train employees on new technology; in one class linked by the network, 800 EDS engineers in 125 different classrooms attended a half day briefing on a new software product.

Implications

In an environment of complex, proprietary networks, each firm wishing to link itself in some way with other organizations has to create a private network; its network will probably not interoperate with networks developed by its trading partners or the firms with which it might form a temporary alliance on some project. The Internet, operating in the United States and much of the rest of the world, and the Minitel system in France are examples of open networks, and they can supply some of the national infrastructure to support IT design variables needed to create the T-Form organization.

However, while the United States lacks infrastructure standards, the situation is not as grim as might appear. Common carriers are trying to win back the business that has gone to proprietary networks. These carriers are offering services like frame relay and asynchronous transfer mode (ATM), high-speed connections that form a wide area network by interconnecting diverse LANs. At the present time, ATM is expensive because of the switching equipment and line speeds involved; if it is successful, prices will certainly fall.

In the meantime, what can a company do to achieve the benefits of networking? There is no need to wait for the development of a national network infrastructure, or information superhighway. A firm can build its own network or form an alliance with a proprietary network provider. It can also explore the Internet as a place to do business, as many firms are doing today. Currently, firms offer information about their products and services on the Internet, usually on a WWW server. The next step is to put catalogues on-line and to process orders. Security still presents problems when processing transactions on the Internet, though several companies offer creative ways to transmit secure payments. At the present time, however, the Internet is not well suited to filling all the roles that a company has for a worldwide network.

The movement toward any kind of standards for networking should encourage the T-Form organization, which relies heavily on the technology of computer networks for forming strategic alliances with partners and for being responsive to these partners (see Table 11.1 for a summary of the variables exemplified in this chapter). The use of *electronic linking and communications, electronic workflows, virtual components, technological matrixing* and remote work, and *electronic customer/supplier relationships* will be considerably easier when businesses can simply plug into a network rather than configure their own. And there is evidence that a network can reduce the

Table 11.1. IT Design Variables and Networks.

IT Design Variable	Example
Electronic linking and communications	Frito-Lay, custom data network
Virtual components	Tax preparers, offering loans based on IRS refunds; purchased networks (from firms like EDS)
Technological leveling	EDS, resulting from its own network
Electronic workflows	IRS and tax preparers
Electronic customer/supplier relationships	CommerceNet; Braun Passot in France
Technological matrixing	EDSNet, for project bidding

need for a managerial hierarchy, helping the T-Form firm to operate with a flat organization structure.

Networks have the potential to transform the way organizations work, facilitating the development of new kinds of business. The development of a national network infrastructure in the United States that features high-speed communications of mixed media, openness, published standards, and ubiquitous access will encourage the development of T-Form structures and operations.

Recommended Readings

Kambil, A., and Short, J. "Electronic Integration and Business Network Redesign: A Roles-Linkage Perspective." *JMIS*, Spring 1994, pp. 59–83.

Lucas, H. C., Jr., Kraut, R., Streeter, L., and Levecq, H. "Minitel: The French National Information Highway." *IEEE Spectrum*, Sept. 1995.

Chapter Twelve

Technologies: The Future That Is Already Here

Chapter One described the T-Form organization, subsequent chapters have illustrated aspects of this kind of structure in more detail, and the last chapter examined the importance of national communications networks in shaping T-Form organizations. Now we can look at the kind of technology the individual T-Form organization requires and at the new technology, still on the horizon, that will make it even easier to use IT variables in organization design.

Technology for the T-Form Organization

It is clear that the T-Form structure involves a variety of communications, so e-mail and groupware are necessary. The firm functions with virtual components, which means that its computers must communicate on-line with computers of its strategic partners. The T-Form organization has extensive electronic linking, then, within the firm and externally. It has electronic connections to customers and suppliers and participates in one or more networks as described in the last chapter.

Within the firm, we can expect to find workstations and local area networks that are connected to wide area networks. Of course, the firm will have automated routine transaction-processing applications. These systems will generate data that can be used for a decision support system (DSS) and an executive information system (EIS). Groupware will support collaboration and coordination within the firm and with external partners.

Is the technology to implement this vision of the firm radical and new? And if not, why have not more firms developed a structure close to the T-Form?

The technology does exist today to create the kind of organization we have been discussing. However, there are many technical and organizational reasons why we do not see a world populated with T-Form organizations. (Organizational reasons are discussed in Chapter Thirteen.)

The Burden of Legacy Systems

From a purely technological standpoint, firms are constrained from moving toward the T-Form organization by their history and installed base of applications. Any firm that has used computers since the 1950s or 1960s has a technology portfolio that has grown over a number of years. Companies find it very difficult and expensive to dismantle their existing stock of technology and adopt entirely new models.

The first commercial use of computers dates back to the 1950s. At that time, all computers were mainframes, and all applications featured batch processing. Users submitted forms to a keypunch department; operators keyed data on the forms into cards. The cards were batched together, and the computer processed them at one time, that is, in one batch.

In the early 1960s, the first on-line systems appeared. Now users could be connected to a computer by means of a terminal and communications lines. The dominant model of computing, however, was still centralized. Users were connected to a single computer or a complex of computers in one location.

Companies developed thousands of applications involving billions of lines of code for mainframe computers. The dominant programming language in the 1960s was Cobol, and IBM had 70 percent of the mainframe market. Mainframe computers have proprietary machine languages. The machine language of an IBM computer differs from the language for a Unisys computer for example. A program written in Cobol is translated to run in the machine language of the computer on which it will be executed. Since IBM has dominated mainframes, a substantial number of Cobol programs have been written for its 370 machine language. One large financial services firm recently reported having over 75,000 active Cobol programs comprising some seventy million lines of code, a significant investment in one language and system.

IBM can add instructions to this 370 instruction set from its fourth generation of computers, but it cannot alter the basic core of instructions used by a tremendous number of existing programs without forcing users to change these programs. You might ask why the industry has not standardized on one version of Cobol, so that programs can be run on many different machines. In fact, there is a standard Cobol, but vendors put additional features beyond the standard into their versions of the language. Also, most modern applications are on-line; they interact extensively with the operating system (that is, the system that supervises the computer and manages its resources—DOS, for example, is the most popular operating system for PCs). Thus, we find billions of lines of what is called IBM MVS Cobol written specifically for IBM's flagship mainframe operating system, MVS.

Change is a common event; organizations are encouraged to be flexible so they can change in response to changing markets and competition. Why should their approach to technology be any different? Unfortunately, it turns out to be very difficult to change computer programs. Programs tend to be poorly documented and hard to understand; often, when changes are needed, the original programmer is no longer with the organization. Programs also interact in strange ways; there can be many unintended consequences from changing code. When Frito-Lay developed its handheld computer systems, it had to change over 900 Cobol programs, a major undertaking.

An organization with a history of mainframe computing is likely to have a number of these *legacy systems*. No one really wants to throw out a system and develop a new one unless the organization totally redesigns the application. Although many IS managers realize that someday these applications will be so old that they have to be replaced, the managers' objective may be to postpone that day as long as possible, until their successors have to worry about it. One popular strategy is to replace terminals connected to a mainframe with PCs and to develop a new interface that "hides" the older system running on the mainframe.

In the late 1960s, technology was changing rapidly. The central processing unit (CPU) had always been the most expensive device to fabricate. However, as integrated circuits were developed, the cost of putting the logic of the computer together dropped dramatically. Kenneth Olsen, founder of DEC, and other MIT engineers saw an opportunity; they developed minicomputers that had a much better price/performance ratio than mainframes. The minis were relatively simple and did not have elaborate input and output capabilities. Minis began to impact mainframe sales, especially when a new application was planned and there were no existing system to consider.

Over time, minis have become more powerful; at the high end, these computers overlap substantially with the capabilities of mainframes. Minicomputers gave rise to a trend toward distributed processing; it was no longer necessary to buy an expensive mainframe in order to provide a remote location with processing power. Of course, soon after remote locations installed minicomputers, they found a need to communicate with mainframes, so companies developed distributed networks of mainframes and minicomputers.

In 1981, IBM legitimized microcomputers by bringing the PC to market. The idea of a personal, relatively inexpensive computer was very appealing; sales of PCs have increased dramatically since their introduction. IBM's decision to publish its standards and to purchase CPU chips from Intel made it possible for a large number of manufacturers to get into the business of making and selling PCs.

Because the base of PCs was growing, software vendors wrote thousands of applications for them, helping the Intel architecture to become dominant.

As the technology advanced, PCs became more powerful, rivaling some small minicomputers. Because the IBM PC architecture dominates business use, millions of users can run the same programs and share information. While the first PCs ran alone on users' desktops, people soon found that they wanted access to data on mainframes, and they wanted to communicate with others in the organization. During the last five years, firms have moved rapidly toward networking their PCs with each other and with other computers. Lotus developed Lotus Notes knowing that most potential customers would have the PCs and network to run it.

Of course, the Apple Macintosh is also a popular microcomputer. However, the Mac has not been able to overcome the huge sales advantage of the PC in business. As a result, Apple joined with IBM and Motorola to develop the PowerPC chip to compete with Intel. In theory, this chip will execute both Macintosh and PC applications. However, it has to do so through a technique called emulation; a combination of hardware and programming makes the PowerPC able to execute Intel instructions. To date, this emulation has not been 100 percent successful; it also slows the speed of the computer, since emulation requires the PowerPC to execute many instructions to carry out one Intel instruction. There are also programs available that will simulate a PC on a Macintosh; these programs work reasonably well, but are even slower than emulation. One Mac model contains an Intel 486 chip to supplement the standard Motorola Mac processor; this machine can run Microsoft Windows and other PC software by switching to the Intel chip. Many experts expect the Mac and IBM PC worlds eventually to merge, so that each company's software can be used on either a PC or a Mac.

You may have run across the term *open system*. The idea of an open system is that you are not tied to a given hardware manufacturer. The term is most often associated with Unix, an operating system that was developed many years ago at Bell Labs. Unfortunately, there are several versions of Unix so program compatibility is less than 100 percent. However, most programs that run under Unix can be moved relatively easily among computers that use this operating system. As a result, the Unix user is not tied as closely to the underlying hardware as is the case for users of many other operating systems. This freedom is especially obvious if you compare Unix to, say, MVS Cobol on an IBM mainframe.

The Client-Server Model

Client-server computing, according to most industry publications and vendors, is expected to become the dominant technological architecture for the future. The client-server model is a network. Each computer in the organization is attached to the network. Some computers on the network are designated as servers; they contain data in files or programs that client computers will access. The client computers are those of the individual users in the firm. Individual users make requests to the servers for their data and/or programs. Servers can be allocated in a variety of ways; you could decide to have a server for each department, or you could dedicate a server to each application, such as customer service.

Client computers will be PCs or a Unix-based computer, such as a Sun. And there are many possibilities for a server. If you read ads from PC vendors, they will argue that the best server is one of their large PCs, possibly a multiprocessor with several CPUs. If you listen to IBM, the mainframe will become your server of choice. At this point, all vendors are trying to endow their computers with the software and communications capabilities to be servers.

While the specific configuration of hardware and software or even the name of the technology architecture is not important when considering the overall T-Form organization, the presence of a network is central. The T-Form organization makes extensive use of electronic linking and communications to develop a flat organization structure with minimal layers of management and to ensure a fast response to problems within the firm or from external services. Today's technological trend is client-server—a trend built around the kind of electronic communications needed by the emerging T-Form organization.

Where Is Your Firm Positioned?

Given this brief history, where does the typical organization stand with respect to technology? Firms can be divided into several technological classes, as illustrated in Table 12.1. The newest firm to adopt technology has the advantage in developing its technological infrastructure. It does not have historical hardware and software or legacy applications to convert. This firm can build a highly networked system featuring workstation clients and servers as needed. Calyx & Corolla is a good example of this kind of firm. It is no coincidence that C&C is the closest example I have found to a T-Form organization; the company started from scratch in terms of business plans and technology.

Companies in the second category in the table also are in a good position to change their organization structure. They either never had legacy systems or they successfully moved to client-server computing by converting their legacy systems to newer technology.

Companies in the bottom row of the table face the biggest challenge. Type A firms are at least moving in a direction that stresses networking and widespread access to computers on the network. Unfortunately, there are still many type B firms. These are the companies that have not kept up with technology and that tend to view IT as a cost rather than an investment. Since installation of some new technology is needed before a firm can change its organization structure, these firms are locking themselves into both old technology and rigid structures. The forecast for such firms is not optimistic.

Table 12.1. Classification of Companies and Their Technology.

Type of Company	Type of Technology
New firms and start-ups	Do not have legacy systems; will develop open networks based on Unix, Windows NT, or entirely on PCs
Technology users for at least a decade but found that they were able to migrate to open systems	Networked environments with hardware and software that do not lock the the firms to a particular hardware vendor; likely users of Unix and/or PCs
Long-time users of technology dating from 1950s and 1960s	Type A: have kept up with technology and have some legacy systems on mainframes but are highly networked and are moving toward the client-server computing model Type B: have predominantly mainframe applications and have not kept up with networking technology

Technology in the Near Term

We have looked at the past and at current directions in technology architecture. What technology will soon be available that will enhance our ability to create T-Form organizations?

Computer hardware continues to expand in capabilities while prices are continually driven down by competition and new R&D. Today's workstations on the desktop are more powerful than mainframe computers of ten years ago and offer far better cost/performance ratios. It is clear that hardware has become a commodity item.

Mainframe computers are becoming multiprocessors, with many of the processors being commodity chips like the PowerPC. These machines, at least those from IBM, will have to emulate the instruction set and software that allow MVS Cobol systems to run. As commodity chips help reduce the price of mainframes (and since mainframe is becoming a pejorative term), in the future, we will probably no longer differentiate among "mainframes," "minis," and "PCs." Possibly, we will go to "small," "medium," and "large" (although probably not "one size fits all") to describe computers.

The actual hardware suppliers who will be popular are hard to predict, though that would be nice to know when purchasing computers today. Certainly the Intel family of PC chips will be a strong contender in the future. With IBM, Motorola, and Apple behind the PowerPC, it is likely this chip will survive, too. HP has its precision RISC architecture, and DEC has staked its future on the Alpha chip. Whether these systems will be major players in the next decade is not as clear.

Relatively new is the PDA, or personal digital assistant. The first models of these devices have been expensive, and they have not offered many features. However, in just a few years, as the technology improves and costs drop, a number of people will be connected to networks through a PDA. These units have limited functional capabilities; for example, they might offer a calendar or agenda, a small spreadsheet package, a notepad, and similar applications. But it is the communications potential of the PDA that is most exciting. Using wireless links, the PDA allows the user to handwrite a note or memo and send it to a colleague's PDA. This kind of electronic linking will make it easier to coordinate employees who are widely dispersed geographically.

On the software side, things are just as confused. It is unlikely that you will develop new applications in MVS Cobol for an IBM mainframe, but what you will change to is less certain. Many client-server applications are being developed using C or C++, a language considered to be "object-oriented." However, this language is not particularly friendly nor easy to modify. Some old-time IS managers claim it costs them 50 percent more to develop client-server applications on Unix using C++ than it does to develop an MVS Cobol application.

However, a number of languages are available that operate at a higher level than C, including Visual Basic from Microsoft and a very high level language called Powerbase. Other vendors are planning to offer similar development tools to increase productivity in building applications. Lotus Notes, as mentioned in Chapter Ten, contains applications development capabilities that users have found to be very productive. And the alliance that Lotus and AT&T have formed to make Notes available on AT&T servers, with slimmed-down Notes client software for $50, has the potential, Lotus believes, for turning Notes into a common system for business-to-business communications.

Just as with applications software, the future of operating systems software is difficult to forecast. Some form of MVS for IBM mainframe applications will have to stay around for many, many years, since it is unlikely anyone will convert the estimated thirty to seventy billion lines of Cobol code in the world right away. Microsoft will continue to expand Windows for the desktop (the next version, Windows95, replaces DOS and is reportedly easier to use than Windows 3.1) and to encourage the use of Windows NT for servers. Unix will be a major competitor for servers as will the OS/2 operating system from IBM. Networking software will help create mixed systems of computers. In the Stern School at New York University, we run PCs with DOS and Windows, Unix clients, Unix servers, and even an odd OS/2 server here and there on the same network. Most of the time, it works!

Networks and communications options are expanding rapidly; but exactly who will own the network you use in the future is not clear. It could be a local telephone company, a cable company, or a long-distance carrier like MCI, Sprint, or AT&T. All want to provide the wire or fiber-optic cable that enters your house or business.

The driving force for these information highways is speed, that is, how much capacity will your line have? Speed is measured several different ways; one common number is bits per second. The twisted pair of wires in a telephone system offers relatively slow speed. Although, engineers have developed equipment to send data over these lines at increasing speeds, today's limits do not allow for full-motion VCR-quality video, which needs about 1.5 million bits per second. For this reason, the telephone companies are planning to install fiber-optic lines to houses or are trying to form alliances with (or purchase) cable TV firms that have high-capacity cables already wired to the home. Eventually, very high speed circuits will be available to firms that need them. The latest development is asynchronous transfer mode (ATM), mentioned earlier; AT&T has an ATM switch that operates at twenty billion bits of data a second. Such capacities should be adequate for most firms.

A complete network is not yet available for communications at these speeds, but it will be in the near future. GTE already offers its ImageSpan system, in which a satellite is used to provide a high-speed distribution system for high-quality graphics. Other satellite-based communications systems are being planned, as described below.

While most of the technology discussed so far in this chapter require wires or cables, for people who no longer have a physical office or who travel frequently, it will be important to avoid the need to plug into a network. These individuals will make use of wireless technology. Cellular phones are an example of a technology that does not require wires, and there are a number of other wireless services available. Two companies, RAM and Ardis, offer wireless connections that cover most of the United States and rely on radio transmission; they are fine for voice and for character-oriented data; they are not adequate for video.

There are at least two ventures planning to develop low-orbit satellite communications systems. Irridium, conceived by Motorola, is the closest to reality. Some sixty-six low-orbit satellites will pass calls among themselves to complete a connection between the origin and destination of the call. Because the satellites are in low orbit, the handset will be smaller and need less power than alternative satellite phone systems. With this system, one would truly have a global communications capability. Microsoft and McCaw

Cellular have proposed a $9 billion system consisting of 840 satellites. This network would carry information from telephone calls to high-resolution medical images and two-way conferences, to and from almost every location on earth.

In the future, there will be even more services that provide electronic communications on a local or global scale. However, the options for communications that exist today are adequate to build the T-Form organization. These options are economically feasible as well.

Given the existing technology, what applications will you be able to run in your firm, applications that will facilitate the T-Form organization? Conferencing software is available now that will let you hold simultaneous discussions with people at different locations. Vendors are also offering videoconferencing facilities, in which participants appear in a window on your workstation, although this technology is currently not inexpensive. Intel's ProShare is one example. Currently, remote users can make a connection in which each site appears in a window on the other computer, and these users can view a document at the same time and work simultaneously on applications like a spreadsheet. Intel has also developed a version of ProShare that lets users on a LAN have a videoconference and share applications without adding a great deal of equipment. The ProShare hardware requires a high-speed phone connection. Soon, LANs will be able to interconnect for conferences.

Lotus and Intel have just formed a partnership in which Lotus will develop Notes products to work with ProShare. Notes currently allows sequential revisions; with new products and ProShare, Notes users should be able to work together on a document or spreadsheet simultaneously; they also could communicate through a voice and video link while working.

An electronic conference without video links is simpler, of course. In a nonvideo environment, you log into a conference and are alerted to new comments on any discussion that you were following. If multiple participants are conferencing at the same time, comments appear on each person's continuously scrolling screen. There is always a record available of the comments that have been made to date. This kind of software makes it easy to conduct remote meetings.

The physical electronic meeting support or group decision rooms and software described earlier are currently available, and some firms already use electronic meetings extensively (to the point that the rooms are always booked). In this mode, all participants need to be physically present.

Paper is the antithesis of electronic communications. Most of us have spent years working on and with paper. Our challenge is to consider electronic storage the natural way of maintaining information and to view paper as one form of display. Imaging systems now allow firms to convert paper documents to electronic format for easy distribution and storage. Recall how Oticon, the Danish hearing aid manufacturer discussed in Chapter Six, scans all incoming documents and then shreds them and how Merrill Lynch images securities and associated documents to facilitate processing and retrieval. The technology is available to move to a less paper dependent though possibly not completely paperless office.

The firm that uses imaging software also needs workflow software. Workflow programs facilitate the routing and processing of documents. For example, if an insurance company that uses image processing receives an application for life insurance, it would scan the application and forward it to a workflow program that manages the application's path through the company. The software would route the application to each individual who needs to review it and would see that all individuals' tasks are completed.

One of the most promising ideas to surface recently is that of *agents*. An agent is a piece of software that does your bidding in some way. For example, you might tell an agent to take a memo you have just composed on your PDA (handheld personal digital assistant) and send it via a wireless modem to a central database for filing. Another agent might call up a stock market data service at 4:30 P.M. everyday and automatically price your stock portfolio at the close of the stock market. An agent might someday contact the people working for you and collect progress reports from them. As yet, we do not have software agents who understand what they are doing, but Artificial Intelligence researchers are working on systems that have limited understanding of a problem domain and could possibly interpret some of the reports from your co-workers.

Some software agents already exist. Hewlett-Packard uses an agent to automate a quarterly wage review for 13,000 sales representatives. Software running on a PC does what twenty administrators have done manually in the past. The agent program dials into the Hewlett-Packard personnel system to get a list of the sales staff working for each of 1,200 sales managers in the United States. The agent e-mails each manager a list for verification and collects any changes by e-mail; it reports these changes back to the personnel system. The agent then repeats the process, but this time, it includes proposed salary changes supplied by management for each sales rep. Managers can approve the changes or alter them by phoning the PC to key in a new piece of data.

AT&T is starting an on-line service called PersonaLink, which is a highway designed for personal electronic agents. As envisioned, the agents on this highway will communicate with other people's agents or with various merchants. The company claims that this system will change the way we conduct commerce and even alter the way people socialize.

The technology that makes AT&T's service possible comes from the software consortium General Magic. This consortium has developed a product called Telescript for programming personal agents to move around a network and complete the tasks their owners assign to them. Magic Cap software is supposed to make programming an agent as easy as filling out a short list of tasks. Currently, agents are capable of looking through junk e-mail and scheduling appointments. In the near future, you should be able to send an agent out with instructions to search the network and look for the cheapest VCR being offered or the lowest-cost vacation package to Europe. One agent is set up to let you communicate with your brokerage firm. The user clicks on an icon, fills in blanks on a list to identify the stock, indicates a price range and an alert trigger, and asks to be paged if a limit is exceeded. The agent then sits inside the brokerage firm's database to wait and search for the event in its task list, at least it waits as long as the customer is willing to pay to have it active!

For PersonaLink to work, merchants will have to sign up to be on the network; they will keep product descriptions and prices on file so that agents can find them. The network will then become a large virtual store containing offers from a variety of merchants, an electronic retail market similar to electronic stock exchanges.

Agents are likely to spread to other networks; they offer an extremely flexible way to establish electronic linking and communications with other firms and individuals. To some extent these agents will automate tasks for the knowledge worker as robots have automated tasks in the factory.

Implications

Today, while we do not yet have one global information superhighway that we can plug into for communications, we have all the other pieces needed to build technology for the T-Form organization. Accessing these resources and setting up a system will be difficult, but the rewards are potentially great. It is the kind of technology described here, highly networked computing and communications, that will make it possible for managers to use IT design variables to create the T-Form organization of the next century.

Recommended Readings

The amount of material on technology is staggering! To keep track of the changes as they continue to occur, you will find periodicals to be your best source of information. Sources such as PC Magazine, PC Week, and technology columns in Business Week and The New York Times are good places to watch for interesting products and trends.

Implications

Recommended Readings

Part Five

Implementing the T-Form Design

The examples we have seen in the previous chapters suggest that at least some firms are moving toward the T-Form organization. However, much of this movement is unconscious or a natural evolution of the application of technology. For the entrepreneur starting a company, use of the IT design variables to create a T-Form organization is one way to improve the chances of a successful start-up. The T-Form is efficient, has a low overhead, and is responsive to customers—all factors important for a new company.

While it is never easy to design an organization, the start-up has a major advantage over existing, traditional firms. The start-up does not have a possibly obsolete technology infrastructure, and it does not have employees with a vested interest in the status quo. It is hard to imagine an entrepreneur starting out to hire bureaucrats; rather, bureaucrats seem to creep into organizations only as they age and grow larger.

Chapter Thirteen offers some advice on the difficult problem of implementing a T-Form organization, especially the challenge of converting a traditional and possibly bureaucratic firm to this new structure. Chapter Fourteen summarizes the characteristics of the T-Form organization and reviews some of the examples in the text that apply to each IT organization design variable.

It is hard to think of a more difficult management challenge than implementing a new form of organization. Yet the twenty-first century is rapidly approaching, and all signs point to it as a time of intense global competition. I strongly believe that the firms that use IT design variables to create a T-Form organization are the ones that will survive and flourish in this new century.

Chapter Thirteen

The Challenge of Change: Converting from Old to New Design

Adopting the T-Form organization is one way to increase your chances for success in the highly competitive global economy that will open the twenty-first century. The most favorable situation for using IT organization design variables is a start-up firm. However, if many of today's existing organizations are to survive, they will have to undergo massive, significant changes. This chapter discusses some strategies for transforming these existing traditional firms.

Benefits and Costs of the T-Form

Previous chapters have presented a number of advantages of the T-Form structure. It encourages:

- A lean organization with the minimal number of employees necessary for the business to function
- A responsive organization that reacts quickly to threats from competitors and changes in the environment
- A minimum overhead organization
- A structure with low fixed costs, due to virtual components, partnerships, and subcontracting
- An organization that is responsive to customers and suppliers
- An organization that is more competitive than firms with traditional structures
- A organization that allows its employees to develop their capabilities and maximize their contributions to the firm

One of the major advantages of the T-Form organization is that it lacks a large number of hierarchical levels. This flat organization is *responsive* because decisions are made quickly; they do not have to pass through many managerial levels. The flat structure and the resulting responsiveness add up to lower overhead than is found in the traditional bureaucratic organization. The end result should be a firm that is more competitive than traditional hierarchical organizations due to its responsiveness and lower operating costs.

There are, however, costs that go along with these benefits.

- The organization has to invest in information technology.
- The organization has to manage its IT.
- Employees have to learn new technologies and constantly update their knowledge.
- Managers have to work with a large span of control.
- Managers have to supervise remote workers.
- The organization has to manage its close relationships with partners and other companies in various alliances.

It is informative to examine these costs in more detail.

Certainly the T-Form organization will require a large investment in information technology for many firms. However, it is not clear that this investment will be any larger than the estimated 30 to 50 percent of U.S. capital expenditures that are currently invested in IT.

Many managers do not feel they are getting a great deal for their current investment in technology, but the kind of IT used for the T-Form organization has a potentially large payoff if it lets you obtain the benefits described in this book. Think of Calyx & Corolla, where a modest investment in communications and order-processing technology allowed the firm to negotiate agreements with many partners, agreements that created a number of virtual components for the firm.

One of the most formidable demands on the T-Form organization is the need to manage technology successfully. It is hard to pinpoint why many organizations do an ineffective job of managing IT. Certainly, information technology is complex. A firm may feel caught between demands for services and large numbers of vendors, all of whom feel their hardware and or software is the solution for the firm. As the last chapter illustrated, technology has gone through many changes in a relatively short period of time. These changes put cost and management pressures on the firm to keep up with systems and equipment.

Firms also are often run by managers for whom technology is a large unknown; they are forced to manage something they do not understand. Often these managers are assisted by subordinates who are technically competent but have little understanding of the needs of the business. Some senior managers react to the challenge of IT by delegating it to a technical manager or chief information officer (CIO); these individuals are often highly paid executives with large budgets and many employees reporting to them. CIOs also tend to have short careers with any given employer, evidence that the job is challenging and difficult to do well.

It is not possible in this book to prescribe in detail how the organization can or should manage technology. In fact, there is little agreement among experts on how to manage IT. However, I have found the following outline for managing technology helpful:

1. Determine and communicate corporate strategy.
2. Develop a plan of how to use information technology. The plan should include:

     A list of opportunities for each component or business unit.

     A vision of how each unit should function and the role of IT in that vision.

     A survey of business processes that are good candidates for major improvement through process reengineering.

     A catalogue of areas for applying IT, including their priority.

3. Create a plan for developing the technological infrastructure:

Plan the hardware/software architecture for each unit, given the constraints of the corporation, that is, the existing technology.

Plan the evolution of the network that will form the backbone of your technology.

Invest in infrastructure.

Investigate the use of standards to facilitate connection and interorganizational systems.

4. Develop ongoing management strategies for IT:

Support users in various parts of the firm and encourage them to work with the technology.

Develop mechanisms for allocating resources to IT.

Encourage innovation and reward it.

5. Manage systems analysis and design:

See that design teams are formed for new projects.

Participate in the design process.

Be sure you understand what IT applications will do.

Review and monitor development projects.

6. Be a user of technology:

Use IT to improve your own productivity.

Use technology to set an example for others.

Another cost in the T-Form organization is that of learning new technology. Products and systems are constantly changing; new releases of PC software like spreadsheet packages seem to average more than one per year. If technology is not upgraded and if employees do not learn new systems, then eventually it becomes difficult to share data with others. And of course, the firm forgoes the improvements in the new version of the packages.

The T-Form organization features a large span of control for most managers; the idea is to substitute electronic for face-to-face communications. Implicit in a large span of control is a degree of trust in subordinates. Electronics alone will not substitute for the close control a manager can exercise over subordinates when he or she has only five or six direct reports. A recent news story on Japanese management included a photo of a large number of workers arranged in two rows of desks, each row facing the other. At the end of the row sat the workers' supervisor, with his desk perpendicular to the workers so that he had them under constant view. Evidently a common feature of Japanese organizations, this physical structure is probably the ultimate in close supervision. The T-Form organization is at the opposite end of the spectrum; it requires managers to give more responsibility to subordinates to do their jobs.

Closely related to the need to adopt a management philosophy stressing subordinate responsibility is the issue of managing remote work. Some T-Form companies are likely to eliminate physical offices for employees who spend a great deal of time traveling or who work from a satellite office or from home. Work-at-home experiments have shown that some managers feel uncomfortable trying to supervise subordinates they rarely see. Remote work, like a large span of control, requires the manager to trust subordinates and, of course, requires subordinates to act responsibly. Some subordinates have reacted negatively to losing their offices and to using part of their homes as offices. They feel the company is forcing its overhead costs onto them. Virtual offices will undoubtedly call for new managerial skills and new relationships between managers and the people reporting to them.

The final management cost of the T-Form organization is that of handling relationships with external firms. These firms might be suppliers or customers, partners in a strategic alliance, or governmental agencies. Calyx & Corolla must deal closely with the partners—the growers and Federal Express—who provide it with virtual components. These partners are a vital part of Calyx & Corolla, but they do not report to its managers. C&C managers have to manage a cooperative arrangement without having the usual tools given a manager: reporting relationships and control over subordinates' salaries. If you own your distribution system, it is easy to tell drivers to leave flowers when no one is home as long as the temperature is above freezing. When your company is a very small part of Federal Express's business, implementing such a policy is much more difficult.

Balancing Costs and Benefits

When trying to implement something new, it is helpful to compare the costs and benefits, as briefly outlined above. Figure 13.1 depicts costs and benefits as forces that affect the changing of the organization structure. The vertical line represents an equilibrium in which costs and benefits balance each other. Moving the line to the right is progress toward the T-Form organization and moving it left is a move toward a traditional hierarchical firm. The benefits of the T-Form organization are on the left pushing toward the right; the costs are on the right pushing left. When managers see the benefits as exceeding the costs, they will move toward the T-Form.

For new organizations like Calyx & Corolla, the advantages of the T-Form should far outweigh its costs; the T-Form fits start-ups very well. A number of Silicon Valley companies employ virtual components and electronic linking; they, too, are well on the way to adopting the T-Form. One start-up, Visioneer, makes a scanning system and software aimed at eliminating paper in the office. The corporate office in Palo Alto is responsible for design, marketing, and sales. The product is manufactured by subcontractors: the circuit board comes from Singapore, and a Boston firm makes the case, tests the product, and ships it to customers. Other partners help write the software. Six sales representatives in the field do not have physical offices; they are linked by mail, voice mail, and cellular phones.

Figure 13.1. Forces in Changing an Organization's Structure.

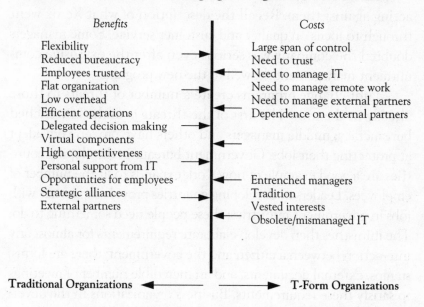

Benefits   *Costs*

Flexibility	Large span of control
Reduced bureaucracy	Need to trust
Employees trusted	Need to manage IT
Flat organization	Need to manage remote work
Low overhead	Need to manage external partners
Efficient operations	Dependence on external partners
Delegated decision making	
Virtual components	
High competitiveness	
Personal support from IT	
Opportunities for employees	Entrenched managers
Strategic alliances	Tradition
External partners	Vested interests
	Obsolete/mismanaged IT

Traditional Organizations ◄——— ———► T-Form Organizations

What are the possibilities of moving more traditional firms toward the T-Form? In addition to the costs discussed earlier, further forces (shown as the last four costs in Figure 13.1) act against the T-Form in hierarchical firms. These forces are "costs" to the current employees of the firm as the T-Form clearly threatens many vested interests.

In traditional firms, a minor restructuring of a department or workgroup will not let the firm enjoy the benefits of the T-Form organization. To move toward the T-Form will require a massive change, one that includes all employees and units of the firm. Management might start in one department or division, but as mentioned earlier, often change will not happen until a critical mass accumulates. E-mail does not achieve its potential if only 50 percent of the firm's staff use it. Customers may be happy to use EDI with one division, then wonder why the rest of the company does not offer electronic linkages.

Massive changes are difficult to carry out; there are many forces acting against them. Recall the description of what Xerox went through to focus on quality and customer service. Some managers doubted the company was serious even after the extensive commitment management showed to the new program.

Major change programs create a number of threats to those already in the firm. The first of the threats is to the entrenched bureaucracy; middle managers and others have proven very adept at protecting their jobs. Government bureaus in developing countries are a good example of how work expands to fit the number of employees. Leaders in developing countries provide supporters with jobs in government ministries; these people need something to do. The ministries then develop elaborate requirements for almost any interaction between a citizen and the government; there are forms, stamps, external documents, and an incredible number of meetings to satisfy these requirements. Business organizations in the developed nations show less of this phenomenon, but I have seen many firms in which layers of management accept documents from lower levels, sign them without adding much value, and pass them to the next highest layer. The T-Form organization does not have jobs for these people. As a result, it is likely that there will be fewer employees; the T-Form organization will require the company to downsize. Clearly downsizing is a threat to existing employees, and it is natural for them to oppose an organizational form that encourages a smaller firm.

A manager committed to the T-Form will also ask fundamental questions about all the tasks performed in the organization. Should we continue to operate a transportation system, or should we contract with outside carriers? Should we eliminate all forms of payment except credit cards and do away with the accounts receivable department? Should we contract out our IS operations? The threat that the firm might make any of these partnerships or alliances is certain to arouse resistance on the part of current employees.

Motivating Organizational Change

It will be very difficult in many traditional firms to create movement toward the T-Form organization. What might motivate such a firm to change structures?

- A merger or acquisition
- A major crisis, for example, substantial losses
- Bankruptcy
- Rebellion by the board of directors
- Legal or regulatory reversal
- A competitor's success

Mergers and acquisitions often result in new management teams. New managers might look at the firm and realize that the situation of integrating two companies is a good time to develop a new overall structure. Unfortunately, sometimes it takes a major crisis to motivate managers; most of the remaining motivational items in the list above might well come under this heading. A rebellion by the board of directors is often a crisis. The chairmen of companies having significant problems have been asked to resign in record numbers in the last few years; powerful chairmen at IBM, DEC, Westinghouse, and GM, among others, have suffered this fate. In a crisis situation, a new manager has a certain amount of leverage for changing the organization.

Bankruptcy is another traumatic event that may well provide the opportunity for a dramatic restructuring of a firm. Unfortunately, the bankrupt firm is at a disadvantage in its efforts to partner with other firms and to form alliances, given the history that put it into bankruptcy in the first place. It may also lack the funds necessary to develop a technological infrastructure. A legal or regulatory reversal may also provide the motivation for a firm to look to the T-Form for a new structure.

A crisis may be the strongest motivation for reorganization. Possibly the second strongest reason is competition. If a firm sees its competitor performing significantly better after having adopted a new structure, it may imitate that competitor. Of course, if enough firms adopt a T-Form structure, that structure will become fashionable, and others will imitate it. But those others will be in the position of catching up with the early adopters.

A Change Program

How should a manager go about trying to create a T-Form organization? Chapter One discussed the steps involved in designing the T-Form organization; in this chapter, we are concerned with actually implementing the design. A design process is conceptual; implementation is the process of creating change in the organization.

Change is one of the most difficult things to bring about. The situation illustrated in Figure 13.1 can be thought of as a force field, with forces acting for and against change. To bring about change, and move the organization from one state, the traditional hierarchical organization, to another, the T-Form, management can either increase the forces for change and/or decrease the forces opposing change. Some general approaches to strengthening the forces for change are given in the following section, but of course, each organization is different and managers must custom tailor these general approaches to specific organizations. Table 13.1 (based on some of the ideas of Nadler and Tushman, 1988) summarizes the key steps and some recommended actions.

The first step is to motivate the change. While some crises may provide enough motivation for action, you may also be able to call attention to less dramatic events to convince everyone that change is needed.

A second step is to accumulate the power and resources necessary to bring about change. It is especially helpful here to have broad support from the board of directors and others who have

Table 13.1. Implementing the T-Form Organization.

Step	Action
Motivate the change	Explain reasons, such as competition and/or falling sales; communicate with everyone in the organization.
Accumulate power and resources	Obtain support from key individuals and groups in the organization; be sure you have the influence and resources to bring about change.
Develop a transition plan	Use a task force to develop the vision for the new organization; describe steps that must be taken to reach a new organization structure; take full advantage of IT design variables.
Manage anxiety	Communicate with employees; consider a groupware rumor mill application; provide outplacement and counseling; involve employees in designing the new organization.
Build IT capabilities	Technology must be in place to enable the T-Form; there is often a lead time for implementing the technology itself before you can make changes in the organization.

influence in the firm. It is likely that a substantial investment will be needed to implement change.

Having a plan for the transition to a new organizational form, the third step, is very important. The plan should provide a road map for action and should be capable of being used to keep employees aware of what is happening. Assembling a task force for developing the plan is a good way to bring employees into the change process and to tap their knowledge for building the new organization. The results of the task force should be widely disseminated. As they work, the members of the task force should be sure to take maximum advantage of the IT design variables discussed in this book.

Employees will experience much anxiety with even the suggestion of a change in the status quo that could alter their jobs or even eliminate them. Nadler and Tushman suggest that one job for management is to manage anxiety in the change process. Involving workers in planning and executing a change program is one way to reduce (although not eliminate) anxiety. On balance, it is a good idea to stress open communications rather than to keep plans secret. However, even when individuals are aware of the company's plans, they may see changes that look very threatening to them. In today's business environment, a responsible firm will provide counseling and outplacement services for employees who are no longer needed. There should be no occasion for people to repeat among themselves stories about the colleague who at 9:30 A.M. was told he would not be needed any more and that he should not plan on being in the office after 4:00 P.M.!

Finally, making the transition to the T-Form organization requires that the firm have adequate technology already in place. You may develop the capabilities needed in-house, or you may turn to outside vendors. At a minimum, you will need a communications network and e-mail. Depending on your business, you may need electronic connections to buyers and suppliers. Some of these links can be purchased through value-added carriers and other service companies. Placing workstations in offices and connecting them into networks is important. Increasingly, it appears that groupware like Lotus Notes will become an important way of managing within the organization and a mechanism for linking to external partners.

The task here is to design your firm's technology so that it will enable, not constrain, your firm's ability to move toward a T-Form organization. Once the technology infrastructure is in place, you can use the IT design variables to develop the structure of the organization.

The following questions can assist you in identifying the IT variables that are likely to be important to your organization design. These questions can be combined with the steps for designing the T-Form organization (see Table 1.1 and Chapter Fourteen) as part of the process of arriving at an appropriate structure for a firm.

1. What are the most significant processes in the organization (for example, order fulfillment, manufacturing, and so on)?
   a. To what extent should these processes be redesigned?
   b. What opportunities do new technologies and IT design variables offer for improving these business processes?
2. Who are our major partners, including customers, suppliers, and others (banks, accountants, law firms, and so on)?
   a. What opportunities are there for *electronic linking and communications* with these organizations?
   b. Where should we try to establish *electronic customer/supplier relationships?*
   c. What additional services can these partners provide? What opportunities are there to create *virtual components?*
3. What should our strategic organization be? Should we be organized by product, by region, or by a combination of factors?
4. What is our competitive strategy? How do IT design variables help us implement this strategy?
5. Given the major processes in our business, how do we assign personnel to be sure these processes are accomplished?
   a. Can we use *technological leveling* to minimize the number of layers in the organization?
   b. Do *production automation* and *electronic workflows* have something to contribute to our business processes?
6. What kind of managerial hierarchy is necessary?
   a. Again, can we use *technological leveling* to reduce layers and broaden the span of control for managers?
   b. Can we use *technological matrixing* to form temporary task forces and workgroups instead of establishing permanent departments and reporting relationships?

The overall objective is to create an organization with a flat structure, flexibility, responsiveness, decentralized decision making, effective communications, links to business partners, and other characteristics of the T-Form structure.

Significant organizational change is a challenge; Machiavelli summed it up over 400 years ago in *The Prince:* "There is nothing more difficult to take in hand, more perilous to conduct, or more uncertain in its success than to take the lead in the introduction of a new order of things."

The major challenge facing managers in the twenty-first century will be to design organizations that take advantage of the IT design variables discussed in this book. Moving toward the T-Form organization will require new ways of thinking for the start-up and massive changes for traditional organizations. While there are many perils to confront in changing an organization's design and structure, there are many organizational benefits to be reaped from the introduction of current and future information technology. Senior managers must decide if these benefits are sufficiently compelling to sustain their organizations through the times of change.

Recommended Readings

Lucas, H. C., Jr. *Information Systems Concepts for Management.* (5th ed.) New York: McGraw-Hill, 1994.

Nadler, D., and Tushman, M. *Strategic Organization Design.* New York: Harper-Collins, 1988.

Chapter Fourteen

The T-Form Reconsidered: Pathways to Success and Competitiveness

This book has described the T-Form organization, a firm based on information technology design variables as well as conventional organization design principles.

The T-Form Organization in Perspective

The T-Form organization has a flat structure made possible through *technological leveling*. Supervision of employees is based on trust because managers have fewer face-to-face encounters with subordinates and colleagues than in today's organization. Managers delegate tasks and decision making to lower levels of management; information systems make data available at the level of management where the relevant decisions are to be made. *Electronic linking and communications* among all levels of employees assure that work is coordinated. Some members of the organization work remotely most of the time and have no permanent office assignment.

Most T-Form organizations will use *technological matrixing* to form temporary task teams focused on specific projects. Technology like e-mail and groupware facilitates the work of these task forces. These temporary work groups may include employees of customers, suppliers, and/or partner corporations.

The T-Form organization's technology infrastructure features networks of computers. Individual client workstations connect over a network to larger computers that act as servers. The network has gateways to national and international networks so that members of the firm can connect with customers, suppliers, and others with whom they need to interact.

T-Form organizations feature *production automation* and *electronic workflows*. They minimize the use of paper and rely extensively on imaging devices and optical data storage. Technology is used to give workers jobs that are as complete as possible rather than being small pieces of tasks; in the office, assembly-line operations for processing documents are converted to a series of tasks that one individual or a small group can perform from a workstation. The firm also adopts and uses electronic agents to perform a variety of tasks over networks.

The T-Form organization has extensive *electronic customer/supplier relationships*. These linkages increase responsiveness, reduce cycle times, improve accuracy, and reduce the amount of overhead involved when firms do business with each other. Suppliers access customer computers directly to learn of customers' needs for materials; suppliers then deliver raw materials and assemblies to the proper location just as they are needed. Customers pay many suppliers as the customer consumes materials, dispensing with invoices and other documents associated with a purchase transaction.

The close *electronic linking* of companies doing business together creates *virtual components*. Traditional parts of the organization appear to exist, but in reality, they exist in a novel or unusual manner. For example, the traditional inventory of raw materials and subassemblies is likely not to be owned or stored by the T-Form manufacturing firm; instead, this virtual inventory exists at suppliers' locations. The subassemblies may not exist in a physical inventory at all; suppliers may build them just in time to provide them to the customer. From the customer's standpoint, however, it appears that all needed components are in inventory because their suppliers are reliable partners in the production process.

Summary of IT Design Variables
and Their Application

Table 14.1 summarizes IT design variables as used by the companies discussed in this book. It shows the rich variety of ways technology has been applied to organization design; there are small start-up companies like Calyx & Corolla and huge global firms like Chrysler and Frito-Lay. For Calyx & Corolla, Oticon, and Mrs. Fields Cookies, IT design variables impact the entire organization. In electronic markets, like those offered by the London Stock Exchange, BZW, and TELCOT, IT design variables have affected the industry and most of its participants so dramatically that competitors have been forced to adopt the technology. In most of the companies, however, IT design variables have been used in isolated parts of the firm. It is hard to say that any of these companies has created a T-Form organization, as yet.

We can draw a number of conclusions from the examples listed in Table 14.1. First, these companies have been successful in *managing* information technology; they have made the decision to invest in IT and then have devoted efforts to seeing that they obtain a return from that investment.

Second, it is clear that all of these variables can be and have been used in successful organization design. As the examples have shown, the variables have been used to change fundamental organization structures and to focus on reengineered operations and customer service and on the creation of new forms of markets.

Finally, these firms appear to have obtained substantial benefits from their new structures. There are examples of:

- Greater flexibility
- Increased efficiency
- Fewer layers of management
- Reduced overhead

Table 14.1. IT Design Variables in Multiple Firms.

IT Design Variable	Example
Electronic linking and and communications	American and United CRSs; Kennametal, Baxter Healthcare, links with customers; TELCOT, NASDAQ, London Stock Exchange, links with market; Frito-Lay, custom data network linking salesforce to company; Mrs. Fields Cookies, links between headquarters and stores; Calyx & Corolla, links between headquarters and growers; House of Windsor Collection, link with Federal Express; EDI at RASCO, Chrysler, and WMS; Otis France, Otisline service order entry and links to service force; Picker, links to field engineers; BZW, links between brokers and market-makers; McKesson, links between drug stores and distribution system; Chase Manhattan and Chemical banks, groupware
Technological matrixing	Lithonia Lighting, agents; Oticon, project task forces; EDSNet, project bidding; Chase Manhattan and Chemical banks, temporary project groups in different locations using groupware
Electronic workflows	Flower Auction Westland, display of flowers being auctioned; Mutual Benefit Life, claims routing; Merrill Lynch, securities routing and retrieval; Lithonia Lighting, bids and quotes; IRS and tax preparers; Calyx & Corolla, flow of orders from customers to order entry to growers; Hewlett-Packard agents; AT&T links with PersonaLink network populated by intelligent agents
Production automation	Mutual Benefit, claims; Merrill Lynch, securities processing; Chrylser, lean production and JIT; WMS, warehouse operations

Table 14.1. IT Design Variables in Multiple Firms, Cont'd.

IT Design Variable	Example
Technological leveling	Merrill Lynch, reduction in SPC employment; Oticon, reduction in management levels at headquarters; EDS, changes resulting from its internal network; Mrs. Fields Cookies, store controller organization; Frito-Lay, reduction in management
Electronic customer/ supplier relationships	American and United CRSs, Rosenbluth Travel, Kennametal, NASDAQ, London Stock Exchange, TELCOT, link buyers and sellers through an electronic market; CommerceNet, service on the Internet; Braun Passot, office supplies in France; RASCO, EDI; Chrysler, EDI, scheduling, and pay-as-built plan; WMS, electronics supplier EDI; Otisline, service order entry and remote elevator monitoring; BZW, broker link; McKesson, multiple links and services to customers; Picker, link to its equipment at customer sites
Virtual components	Kennametal, tool inventory; Baxter, stockless hospital; Oticon, shifting departments and task forces; Tax preparers, offering IRS refunds; purchased networks (like those from EDS); Calyx & Corolla, for production, inventory, distribution and sales; Chrysler, suppliers' inventory; FedEx, for the House of Windsor Collection; BZW, electronic market; McKesson, inventory for pharmacies

- Better customer service
- Reduced cycle times
- Improved operations
- Increased revenues
- Enhanced decision making
- New services and lines of business
- Alliances with suppliers and customers
- Reduced paper processing and fewer manual procedures

For employees, these firms should be a more exciting and less frustrating place to work compared with traditional hierarchical firms. The employee, assisted by technology, can be more responsive to co-workers, customers, and suppliers. When employees have more responsibility, they can execute their ideas without the inertia found in a bureaucracy. One would expect to find enthusiasm and high levels of morale in companies that take advantage of IT design variables.

Overall, the firms discussed in this book have become stronger competitors. They demonstrate that IT design variables can be used *to transform the organization*. These companies provide confidence that managers can create T-Form organizations that will be dynamic, exciting, and aggressive competitors in the twenty-first century.

Steps in Designing the T-Form Organization

At this point, managers who are interested in exploring the use of IT and conventional design variables to create the T-Form organization, can review the design steps recommended in Chapter One.

Step 1: Recognize that the physical and logical structures of an organization are separate. We have seen a number of examples of firms in which the logical structure differs from the physical structure.

Calyx & Corolla has a virtual manufacturing plant (growers) and a virtual delivery system (Federal Express). Accounts receivable are processed by credit card companies.

Step 2: Develop a corporate strategy. A firm needs a strategy, a sense of what it is trying to achieve, and a plan for implementing the strategy. Chrysler's most recent corporate strategy, for example, has been to become the low-cost producer and to emphasize quality of design and value. It currently has the highest profits per car of the three Detroit automakers. Chrysler has invested heavily in IT to implement this strategy.

Step 3: Identify processes. Calyx & Corolla did an excellent job of identifying the different processes needed to operate its business. The company then determined the best way for each process to function smoothly. On a smaller scale, Merrill Lynch examined its securities processing operation and reengineered it to achieve major savings and improvements in service.

Step 4: Integrate classical design steps with IT design variables. IT design variables alone are not sufficient to design an organization. Management still has to be concerned with such design issues as strategic grouping, structure (for example the definition of organizational subunits), work processes, communications, and interorganizational relations. However, the message of this book is that IT design variables provide many options in addition to the traditional ways of organizing.

Step 5: Design the logical structure of the organization. The logical structure of the organization is likely to look very traditional; it represents what employees and customers think they see. It is the virtual corporation.

Step 6: Design the physical structure of the organization. Using the IT design variables discussed in Chapter Four, the designer creates an efficient, low-overhead organization that may not resemble its logical form. However, the IT design variables do generate the logical view the firm wants to present to the world.

Step 7: Plan for temporary task forces and matrix management. IT makes matrix management and temporary task forces much more attractive. Oticon uses temporary task forces and technological matrixing very effectively to allocate human resources to whatever project has priority at any given time.

Step 8: Focus on key decisions that provide choice in organization design. After identifying processes, the question for management is should we operate this process ourselves or form an alliance with someone else to provide the process? Do our employees have to be physically located together or can they work more effectively from different locations? Do they need offices at all?

Step 9: Design tasks. It is best to let individual employees and groups of workers design their own tasks to the greatest extent possible. Management should make information technology available to workers to assist in developing tasks. In some instances, such as the design of a factory, experts will be needed to join employee teams in task design.

Step 10: Build or buy a technological infrastructure. What kind of technology does the organization need if the T-Form organization design is to succeed? Typically, the firm will need networked computers, workstations for information workers, and the ability to connect electronically with suppliers and customers. This technology infrastructure may be purchased and then managed internally, or the organization may turn to outside service firms to provide the appropriate technology. Management must have confidence in the technology and the ability of the organization to take advantage of it. A high level of technological competence is a prerequisite for the use of IT design variables in structuring the organization.

Step 11: Use compensation policy to help achieve goals. Compensation is one of the most important traditional organization design variables when it is used by managers to reward behavior that they want to encourage. For example, you may want to provide a bonus for employees who are willing to give up their physical offices or special rewards for an electronically matrixed task force when it finishes a project. A group bonus may be appropriate to encourage the sharing of information through groupware.

Step 12: Trust workers and lead through influence. The T-Form organization features few hierarchical levels and distributed decision making. By its very nature, it makes close supervision difficult or impossible. With large spans of control and employees who work remotely, the manager must provide guidance and monitor progress rather than supervise closely. As a result, managers have to trust subordinates and can lead the organization only through influence and coaching. For many managers who are used to providing close supervision, the trust needed for the T-Form organization may not exist naturally.

The Importance of Getting Started

As we discussed in the last chapter, it will be easier to construct a T-Form organization from scratch; the start-up firm will find the low overhead and responsiveness of this structure appealing. Moving existing organizations toward the T-Form is more of a challenge. You have to be willing to ask if current functions are needed and to determine whether different layers of management do work that adds value to the firm's output.

In the end, it will be competition that forces firms toward the T-Form. In the twenty-first century, companies will continue to be under relentless cost pressures; managers will have to focus on providing better service to customers and on driving costs out of their business. The T-Form organization substitutes technology for functions that have frequently been done by a human bureaucracy. While substituting technology capital for this labor will create dislocations in employment, the failure of an inefficient and uncompetitive firm creates even more unemployment. In most instances, technology will do a better job than the bureaucracy it replaces.

Thus, while the T-Form organization may at first result in employee surpluses and layoffs, it should help firms remain competitive in a world economy. On the positive side, the T-Form organization does more to empower employees than traditional structures since T-Form employees are expected to take responsibility for tasks. These employees will be better prepared for higher-level jobs since they will gain significant experience in each different position they hold in the firm.

It is always dangerous to be a pioneer and adopt some new idea first. Yet there would seem to be first-mover advantages as well to adopting the T-Form before your competition. An organization cannot transform itself overnight; it takes time to develop the needed technology and to restructure the firm. If you do not begin this process, a competitor or start-up will, taking the risks but also gaining many advantages, possibly including market share.

The T-Form organization is a structure created to obtain the benefits offered by information technology design variables. The challenge for management is, first, to recognize that the design of information technology and the design of organizations have become the same task and, second, to implement the T-Form organization in order to be competitive in the twenty-first century. Are you and your organization ready to start?

Glossary

Agents: "Intelligent" software modules that perform some task for their human owner, like wandering through a network looking for a particular product for sale.

Algorithm: A procedure for accomplishing some task; computer programs are often described as consisting of various processing algorithms.

Analog: Resembling something; analog voice communications, for example, represent voice as a continuous wave form.

ANSI: American National Standards Institute; ANSI develops industry standards for a number of technologies.

Artificial intelligence (AI): The ability of a computer to simulate different aspects of human behavior; also, the field that develops such programs.

Asynchronous transfer mode (ATM): A very high speed digital communications service that is likely to become standard for connecting different computer networks over medium to large distances.

Bit: A 0 or a 1 (a *binary digit*); computers process information in bits, and data are sent over digital communications lines as bits.

CAD/CAM: Computer-aided design/computer-aided manufacturing; using a computer to help design and then fabricate parts.

Cellular: Using small geographical areas (cells) in wireless communications; signals are carried at low power so that the same frequency can be reused in each cell; computers "hand off" calls to new areas as a caller travels from one cell to the next.

Central processing unit (CPU): The part of the computer that controls its operations; the CPU contains the logic of the machine. In PCs, the CPU is generally on a single chip or a small set of chips (Intel makes the 486 and Pentium chips, which are CPUs).

Character: A letter, such as an "a," or some other symbol stored as a code consisting of seven or eight bits; most programs (for example, word processors) process data in characters.

Chip: A small (6 mm x 6 mm) piece of material, generally silicon, with various electronic components on it; the number of components can easily exceed one million.

CIO: Chief information officer.

CISC: Complex instruction set computers; the original strategy for developing processors featuring microprogramming and a large variety of instructions (see also **RISC**).

Client-server: A technology architecture in which some programs and most databases reside on a large computer, a server, that is connected to user workstations; workstations access the server for programs and data and, possibly, for communications purposes.

Cobol: Common *business* oriented *language*; a popular business computing language used heavily on mainframe computers.

Digital: Represented as a digit, usually a 0 or a 1.

DOS: The *disk operating system* used on most IBM personal computers.

EDI: Electronic *data* (or *document*) *interchange*, a system that allows communicating organizations to replace paper in transactions with electronic connections and transmission of data.

Emulation: The use of a combination of hardware and software to make one computing device perform like another.

Expert system: An application of Artificial Intelligence in which a system captures the expertise of a human and makes it available to others.

Fiber optics: Thin strands of glass fiber that carry data as a series of light pulses representing binary digits (0's and 1's).

Firmware: An algorithm or process that is part way between software and hardware; for example, a well-understood program that has been encoded on a chip to make it run faster.

Gopher: A server on the Internet that provides character-oriented information in an easy-to-access manner.

Groupware: Programs used on a computer network to facilitate the sharing of information and communications among members of a group who have a common task in a shared environment.

Hardware: Physical devices.

Hypertext: A system of embedding references in an electronic text so that a user can, if he or she so chooses, follow a topic through a series of documents, possibly stored on different computers.

Icon: A small graphical representation of a program or command that is displayed on a user's computer screen; clicking on the icon with a mouse causes the program to execute or some action to be taken.

Image: Information stored in a form that is more like a photograph than like coded characters; an image might be represented by a resolution of 300 dots per inch or 300 x 300 dots per square inch; see **character.**

Information technology (IT): The combination of computers and communications, including all types of computers from desktop workstations to supercomputers and all types of networks; also fax machines and pagers and communication modes like cable, satellite, and wireless.

Integrated circuit: Many interconnected electronic circuits produced on a single silicon chip; integrated circuits made possible today's computers consisting of processor chips and memory chips.

Internet: A worldwide network linking millions of users on their own networks (that is, a network of networks), at first used for exchanging information among scientists and academics, more recently also used commercially. Suggested by some to be the beginning of a national and international information superhighway.

JIT: Just-in-time; applied mainly to manufacturing inventory; a system in which parts arrive just before they are needed for assembly into a product.

Legacy system: Generally refers to an old mainframe application that has not been updated; typically, it would be very costly to reprogram, and yet the system is probably outdated.

Local area network (LAN): A number of computers and other devices connected together in a small local area, such as one floor of a building or an entire building; increasingly, LANs are being linked to form **wide area networks.**

Machine language: The language the computer hardware is actually capable of executing; computer programming languages have to be translated into machine language.

Mainframe: The original kind of computer; associated today with large computers using proprietary hardware and software and often having cost/performance ratios that are worse than smaller computers.

Microprogramming: Breaking down the machine language instructions of a computer into even finer steps; used to create special, often complex instructions.

Minicomputer: A computer originally developed to compete with mainframes, offering fewer features but a better cost/performance ratio; increasingly called a midrange computer.

Modem: A device to send digital data over analog telephone lines.

Mosaic: A very friendly program to access information on the Internet; it displays graphic images readily.

Multiprocessor: A computer with more than one central processing unit; it provides high performance.

MVS: The most popular IBM mainframe operating system (see **operating system**).

Network: A number of communications devices and often computers connected together via communications lines and/or satellites.

Object-oriented: Used to describe a systems development and programming philosophy that views system components as objects that programs manipulate; advocates claim that object-oriented programming will save development time, effort, and cost.

Operating system: A supervisory program that controls the resources of the computer (see **DOS**).

Optical disk: A disk that holds a great deal of data, which is "burned" on with a laser. Most of today's optical disks can be written once and then read many times.

Packet switching: A communications transmission method in which a device breaks a message up into standard-sized "packets," each with an address; the packets are sent via the best available path through a network to their destination.

Personal computer (PC): The IBM PC and its clones; desktop machines with commodity processor chips, producing the most favorable cost/performance ratio of contemporary computers.

Recognition: The process of converting scanned images, represented by patterns of dots, into the character codes of a computer (see **character**).

RISC: Reduced *instruction set computers*: computers using a very simple architecture to speed computations (see **CISC**).

Scanning: The process of "reading" or converting a paper document for storage in a computer; logically like taking a picture of a document.

Software: Programs or logical statements that give instructions to computer hardware.

Technology infrastructure: The shared technology in a firm that is used by all employees (for example, communication networks), as opposed to a system developed for an individual or small group.

Unix: A popular operating system first used on minicomputers; it is now available on a number of computers, which makes programs running under Unix easier to move among machines.

Virtual: Something that appears to exist in a particular way but does not exist that way in reality. For example, a group of workers may appear from an organization chart to be co-located in a physical department, but each member may actually be in a different location, and work may be accomplished through electronic communications.

Virtual reality: A technologically simulated world or situation; often used in games but also in industry and medicine. A flight simulator is an example of the use of virtual reality.

Wide area network (WAN): A network that spans a large geographical area, such as several sites in a city or a number of sites in a country.

Windows: (1) A graphical user interface from Microsoft that runs on top of DOS on personal computers; (2) in general, a user interface with multiple boxed areas (windows), each devoted to some activity; windows may be visible, tiled, overlapped, or reduced to an icon.

Wireless: Communication that does not require wires (as a conventional telephone does for example); using radio frequencies for personal communications is an example of a wireless system.

Workstation: A powerful computer generally assigned to one user; a desktop computer, usually at least an Intel 486 processor or better or a Sun Workstation; the workstation should have windowing software.

World Wide Web (WWW): A series of links among related topics stored on computers on the Internet; requests to follow a topic through different screens are handled automatically, and the user does not know that he or she is moving from one computer to another.

X.12: A standard for interchanging data among companies, developed by the American National Standards Institute (ANSI).

References

Addonizio, M. "Chrysler Corporation: JIT and EDI (A)." Case study. Boston: Harvard Business School, 1992.

Applegate, L. "The Frito-Lay Consolidated." Case study. Boston: Harvard Business School, 1993.

Applegate, L., and Stoddard, D. "Chemical Bank: Technology Support for Cooperative Work." Case study. Boston: Harvard Business School, 1993.

Bell, T. "Bicycle on a Personalized Basis." *IEEE Spectrum*, Sept. 1993, pp. 32–35.

Berkley, J. "Lithonia Lighting." Case study. Boston: Harvard Business School, 1992.

Bjorn-Andersen, N., and Turner, J. "Creating the 21st Century Organization: The Metamorphosis of Oticon." Paper from the IFIP Working Group 8.2 Conference, Ann Arbor, Mich., Aug. 1994.

Boynton, A. "RASCO: The EDI Initiative." Case study. Charlottesville, Va.: Darden Graduate Business School Foundation, 1990.

Brokaw, L. "Twenty-Eight Steps to a Strategic Alliance." *Inc.*, Apr. 1993, pp. 96–104.

Business Week, Mar. 1, 1993.

Clemons, E., and Row, M. "McKesson Drug Co.: Case Study of a Strategic Information System." *JMIS*, Summer 1988, pp. 36–50.

Clemons, E., and Row, M. "Information Technologies at Rosenbluth Travel." *JMIS*, Fall 1991, pp. 53–79.

Clemons, E., and Weber, B. "London's Big Bang: A Case Study of Information Technology, Competitive Impact and Organizational Change." *JMIS*, Spring 1990, pp. 41–60.

Clemons, E., and Weber, B. "Barclays de Zoete Wedd's TRADE: Evaluating the Competitive Impact of a Strategic Information System." Working Paper no. 89–03–08, The Wharton School, University of Pennsylvania, 1991.

Copeland, D. "Flower Auction Westland: The COSMOS Project." Case study. London, Ont.: University of Western Ontario, 1991.

Copeland, D., and McKenney, J. "Airline Reservations Systems: Lessons from History." *MIS Quarterly*, Sept. 1988, p. 353–370.

Datamation, Feb. 15, 1993, p. 15.

Duliba, K., Kauffman, R., and Lucas, H. C., Jr. "Airline CRS, Agency Automation Strategies and the 'Halo' Effect." Center for Research on Information Systems Working Paper no. IS-94–3, Stern School, New York University, 1994.

Federal Register, Sept. 22, 1992, *57*(184), pp. 43780–43837.

"Frito-Lay's Speedy Data Network." *The New York Times,* Nov. 8, 1990.

Gould, R. M., and Stanford, M. *Revolution at Oticon A/S (A&B).* Lausanne, Switzerland: IMD, 1994.

Hammer, M. "Reengineering Work: Don't Automate, Obliterate." *Harvard Business Review,* July-Aug. 1990, pp. 104–112.

Hammer, M., and Champy, J. *Reengineering the Corporation.* New York: Harper-Business, 1993.

Harrington, L. "Driving Down Inbound Costs." *Traffic Management,* Nov. 1990, pp. 43–48.

"In the Mailbox, Roses and Profits." *The New York Times,* Feb. 14, 1992.

Jarvenpaa, S., and Ives, B. "The Global Network Organization of the Future." *JMIS,* Spring 1994, pp. 25–57.

Kambil, A., and Short, J. "Electronic Integration and Business Network Redesign: A Roles-Linkage Perspective." *JMIS,* Spring 1994, pp. 59–83.

Kearns, D., and Nadler, D. *Prophets in the Dark: How Xerox Reinvented Itself and Beat Back the Japanese.* New York: HarperBusiness, 1992.

"Kennametal Finds the Right Tools." *The New York Times,* Apr. 28, 1992.

Kirkpatrick, P. "Why Microsoft Can't Stop Lotus Notes." *Fortune,* Dec. 12, 1994, pp. 141–146.

Leavitt, H., and Whisler, T. "Management in the 80's." *Harvard Business Review,* Nov./Dec. 1958, p. 41.

Lindsey, D., Cheney, P., Kasper, G., and Ives, B. "TELCOT: An Application of Information Technology for Competitive Advantage in the Cotton Industry." *MIS Quarterly,* Dec. 1990, pp. 347–357.

Loebbecke, C., and Jelassi, T. *Staying at the Top with Otis Elevator: Sustaining a Competitive Advantage Through IT.* Fontainebleau, France: INSEAD, 1992.

Lucas, H. C., Jr. *Information Systems Concepts for Management.* (5th ed.) New York: McGraw-Hill, 1994.

Lucas, H. C., Jr., and Baroudi, J. "The Role of Information Technology in Organizational Design." *JMIS,* Spring 1994, pp. 9–23.

Lucas, H. C., Jr., Berndt, D., and Truman, G. "Reengineering: A Framework for Evaluation and Case Study of an Imaging System." *Communications of the ACM,* in press.

Lucas, H. C., Jr., Kraut, R., Streeter, L., and Levecq, H. "Minitel: The French National Information Highway." *IEEE Spectrum,* Sept. 1995.

Lucas, H. C., Jr., and Olson, M. "The Impact of Information Technology on Organizational Flexibility." *Journal of Organizational Computing*, Jan. 1994, pp. 155–176.

Malone, T., Yates, J., and Benjamin, R. "Electronic Markets and Electronic Hierarchies." *Communications of the ACM*, June 1987, pp. 484–497.

Mintzberg, H. *On the Nature of Managerial Work.* New York: HarperCollins, 1973.

Mintzberg, H. *The Structuring of Organizations.* Englewood Cliffs, N.J.: Prentice-Hall, 1979.

Nadler, D., and Tushman, M. *Strategic Organization Design.* New York: Harper-Collins, 1988.

Orlikowski, W., and Gash, D. "Technological Frames: Making Sense of Information Technology in Organizations." Working Paper no. 3627–93, Sloan School, MIT, 1993.

Ostrofsky, K. "Mrs. Fields Cookies." Case study. Boston: Harvard Business School, 1988.

PC Week, Feb. 20, 1989.

Porter, M. *Competitive Strategy.* New York: Free Press, 1980.

Richman, T. "Mrs. Fields' Secret Ingredient." *Inc.*, Oct. 1987, pp. 65–72.

Rifkin, G. "Digital Blue Jeans Pour Data and Legs into Customized Fit." *The New York Times*, Nov. 8, 1994.

Short, J., and Venkatraman, N. "Beyond Business Process Redesign: Redefining Baxter's Business Network." *Sloan Management Review*, Fall 1992, pp. 7–21.

Vogel, D. R., and others. "Electronic Meeting System Experience." *JMIS*, Winter 1988–1989.

Wallace, S. "Experts in the Field." *Byte*, Oct. 1994, pp. 86–96.

Wilke, J. "Computer Links Erode Hierarchical Nature of Workplace Culture." *The Wall Street Journal*, Dec. 9, 1993.

Williamson, O. *Markets and Hierarchies.* New York: Free Press, 1975.

Womack, J., Jones, D., and Roos, D. *The Machine That Changed the World: The Story of Lean Production.* New York: Harper Perennial, 1990.

Index

A

ABZ, 45–50; failure to use IT, 146–148
Agents, on networks, 10–11, 209–211
Airline CRS, 61–64, 75–79
American Airlines SABRE system, 61–64, 75–79
ANSI X.12 EDI standard, 141–142, 184
ASEA Brown Boveri, 75
Asynchronous Transfer Mode, 194
AT&T Notes, 184
AT&T Personalink, 210–211

B

Baxter Healthcare, 9; electronic market, 93–95
BZW electronic exchange, 155–157

C

Calyx & Corolla, 9, 133–136
Chase Manhattan Bank, 170
Chemical Bank, 170–172
Chrysler, 9; JIT, 144–146
Client-server model, 202–203
Cobol, 198–200
Compensation, 19
Computer processor architectures, 205
Customer-driven firm, 74
Cycle time reduction, 74

D

Decision making, decentralized, 7
Differentiation, 74

E

Economost system, 159–162
EDGAR, 189

E

EDI, 8, 139–142, 183–184
EDSNet, 193–194
Electronic communications, 36, 85–86, 99–100, 135–137, 148–150, 162–164, 175–177, 194–196, 232–233
Electronic cotton market. See TELCOT
Electronic customer/supplier relationships, 36, 85–86, 99–100, 148–150, 162–164, 194–196
Electronic Flower Market, 98–99
Electronic linking, 35, 85–86, 99–100, 136–137, 148–150, 162–164, 175–177, 194–196, 232–233
Electronic markets, 91–93
Electronic securities markets, 95–96
Electronic workflows, 36, 99–100, 120–121, 136–137, 194–196, 232–233
Executive information system, 132

F

Federal Express: at Calyx & Corolla, 135–136; and the House of Windsor, 148
Flexibility: definition of, 56; impact of IT on, 56–58; and IT at the airlines, 61–64; and IT in the securities industry, 64–67; paradox, 58–59; second-order impacts, 59–61
Frito-Lay hybrid organization, 130–133
FTP, 190

G

Global competitor, 74–75
Gopher server, 190
Group meeting rooms, 174–175
Groupware, 167–169; impact of, 172–174

H

Hand-held computer project. *See* Frito-Lay
HTML or Hypertext Markup Language, 191

I

Infrastructure, 179–180
Internet, 188–192
IRS, and electronic filing, 192–193
IT design variables, concept of, 32–33
IT management guidelines, 217–218

J

Just-in-time (JIT), 142–143; at Chrysler, 144–146

K

Kennametal, Inc., 83–84

L

LAN, 182
Lean production, 142–144; at Chrysler, 144–146
Leavitt, H., 43
Legacy systems, 198–202
Levi Strauss, 158
Light*Link system. *See* Lithonia Lighting
Lithonia Lighting, reengineering the firm, 118–120
Logical organization structure, 7, 12–16
London Stock Exchange, 96
Low-cost producer, 74

M

Macintosh, 201
McKesson, 159–162
Mainframes, 198–199
Managerial work, 165–167
Market niche focus, 74
Markets, 87–93; cost of, 88–89; hierarchies, 90–91
Matrix management, 6
Merrill Lynch: reengineering the SPC, 105–114; scanning and imaging at, 110—111
Minicomputers, 200
Minitel, 185–188; business applications, 187–188
Mintzberg, H., 29, 165–167

Mosaic, 21
Mrs. Fields Cookies, 125–130
Mutual Benefit Life, reengineering at, 104–105
MVS, 199

N

Nadler, D., 30–32
NASDAQ, 65–66, 95
Negotiated organizations, 39–40
Network trends, 206–208
New York Stock Exchange, 66
Notes, 168–169
NUMI GM–Toyota joint venture, 143–144

O

Open systems, 201–202
Operating systems, 206
Organization design: definition of, 29–30; example of, 45–50; preparation for, 53–55
Oticon: reengineering the firm, 114–118; scanning at, 117; spaghetti organization at, 115–116
Otis Elevator France, 152–153

P

Panasonic bicycles, 158–159
Pay-as-built program, 145
PDA (personal digital assistant), 205
People: in design, 11–12, 42–45; support of, with technology, 167
Personal computers, 200–201
Physical organization structure, 7, 12–15, 16–17
Picker International, 153–155
Pitfalls in design, 55–56
Porter, M., 73–74
PowerPC, 201
Production automation, 35–36, 120–121, 148–150, 232–233

Q

Quality, 75

R

RASCO, 140–142
Recognition, of scanned images, 110–111
Reengineering, 8, 15–16; definition of, 101–103; and IT design variables,

103–104; questions to ask in design,
120
Right-sizing, 75
Rosenbluth Travel, 80–83

S

Scenario of twenty-first century firm,
20–25
Span of control, 5
Strategic alliance, 9–10
Strategic grouping in design, 30–32
Strategy, 15, 73–75

T

Tasks, design of, 9
Technological leveling, 35, 120–121,
136–137, 175–177, 194–196,
232–233
Technological matrixing, 36, 120–121,
175–177, 194–196, 232–233
Technology: forecast, 204–211; infrastructure, 10, 18–19
TELCOT, 96–97
Telephone networks, 181–183
T-Form organization: benefits and
costs of, 215–220; a change program
for, 224–228; characteristics of, 5–11,
229–231; forces for and against,
220–222; motivation for adoption
of, 223–224, 237–238; overall bene-

fits of, 231–234; questions to guide
design of, 227; steps in design of,
12–20, 234–237
Traditional design variables, 33–34
Traditional organizations, 40–41
Trust, 19–20
Tushman, M., 30–32

U

Unix, 201–202

V

Vertically integrated conglomerates, 41
Video conferencing, 208
Virtual components, 8–9, 34–35, 85–86,
99–100, 120–121, 136–137, 148–150,
162–164, 194–196, 232–233
Virtual organizations, 37–39

W

WAIS, 190
WAN, 182
WMS, 147–148
World Wide Web, 190
Worldwide Group. See Scenario of
twenty-first century firm

X

Xerox, 51–52, 151–152